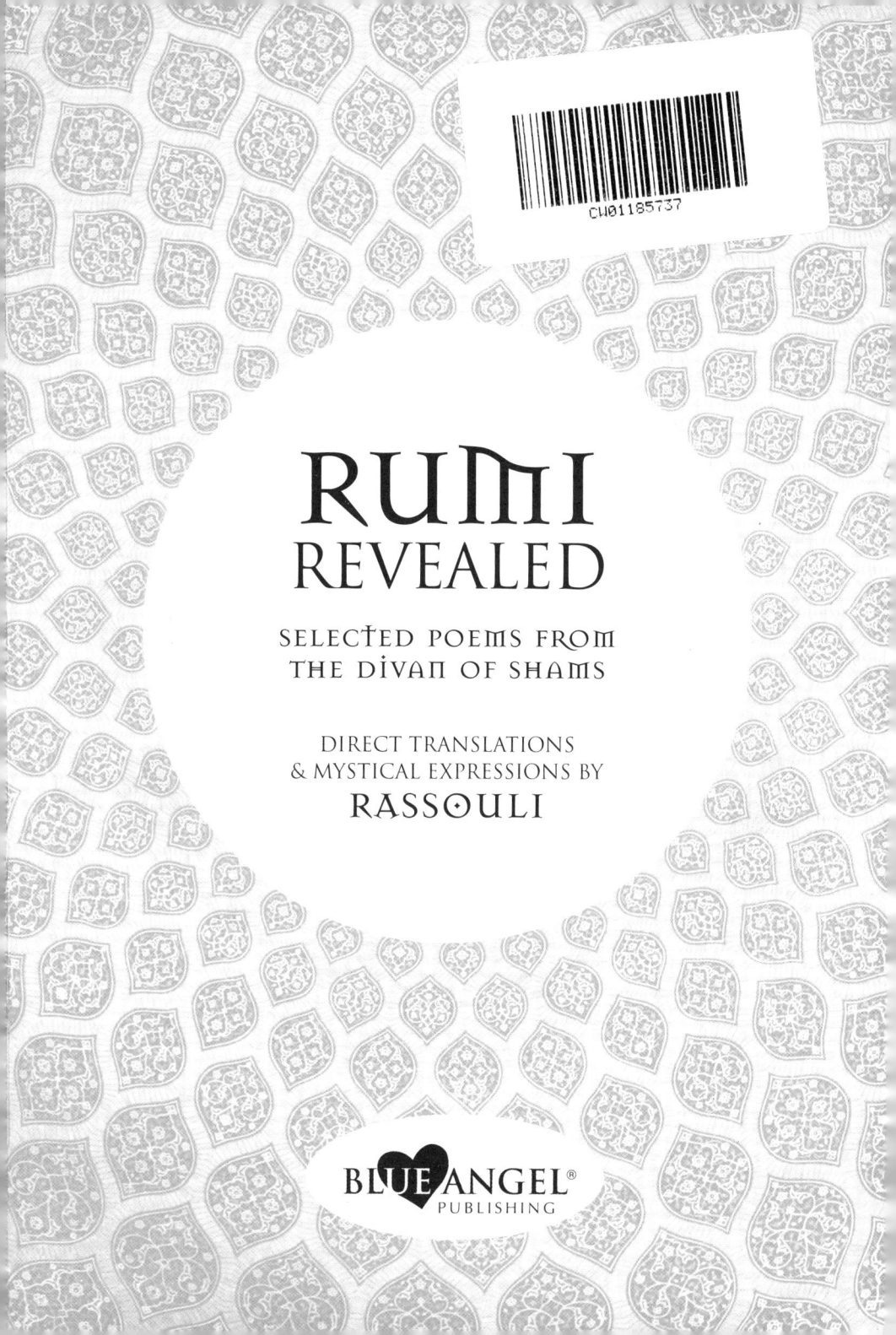

# RUMI
## REVEALED

SELECTED POEMS FROM
THE DIVAN OF SHAMS

DIRECT TRANSLATIONS
& MYSTICAL EXPRESSIONS BY
RASSOULI

BLUE ANGEL®
PUBLISHING

## RUMI REVEALED

Copyright © 2015 Rassouli
www.rassouli.com

All rights reserved.
Other than for personal use, no part of this book may be reproduced in any way, in whole or part without the written consent of the copyright holder or publisher.

Published by Blue Angel Publishing®
80 Glen Tower Drive, Glen Waverley
Victoria, Australia 3150
Email: info@blueangelonline.com
Website: www.blueangelonline.com

Blue Angel is a registered trademark of Blue Angel Gallery Pty. Ltd.

ISBN: 978-1-922161-38-3

*Don't ask me
to define love!
Don't ask anyone to define love!
Ask love to define love.*

*When it comes to describing,
love is like a cloud raining pearls.
Love has no need for my description,
or those of a hundred others like me.*

*Love is the description of Love.*

*Love is not for the frail
and slumbering crowd.
Love is for heroes and the greats.*

Molana Jalal Uddin Rumi

# FOREWORD

Rumi! Mention of his name alone induces a luminous glow on the faces of those who have been touched by his rapturous poetry, for Rumi and divine love are synonymous. Rassouli's gifted translation of Jalal Uddin Rumi's *Divan of Shams*, accompanied by his in-depth interpretations, just like his art, transports the reader to ancient Persia, to a Sufi world whose poetry, music, and dervish dance were suffused with divine intoxication. And, as Rassouli reminds us, the dervish-energy of Rumi's poetry is as available to us today as it was when it was written over 700 years ago.

That being said, what is its practical value to those of us living in the twenty-first century? It is precisely this: Our innate longing to know our true essence as Love—God's only religion—is roused, awakened. In our high-tech, low-touch society, Rassouli has done a great service in presenting to the world a body of work that can be called a divine disturbance because it shakes us from our hard-heartedness, our lives of sterile consumerism and entices us into an inner exploration of authentic intimacy with the Ineffable.

The source of Rumi's and Rassouli's inspiration is one and the same: the Beloved, the stuff out of which we are created, that in which we live, move and have our being. Fortunate are we that friends and students recorded Rumi's ecstatic illuminations, and grateful should we be to a translator such as Rassouli, whose deep inner attunement to Rumi's spirit has produced the precious book you now hold in your hands. Drink richly from it, and then drink some more until the entrancing world of this intoxicated lover of God embraces your own spirit in an ecstatic dance of union with the Beloved.

**Michael Bernard Beckwith**
Founder, Agape International Spiritual Center

# contents

Foreword 5
Preface 9
Introduction 13
Rumi's Life 19

Transformation 25
*Poem No. 1393* 30
Power of Love 33
*Poem No. 1374* 36
Divine Love 38
*Poem No. 2138* 41
Longing for Love 44
*Poem No. 441* 48
Spring of Love 52
*Poem No. 536* 55
Spirit of Love 57
*Poem No. 2429* 59
Attraction of the Beloved 62
*Poem No. 3* 65
Caressed by the Beloved 68
*Poem No. 46* 71
Union of Love 73
*Poem No. 1397* 76
Garden of the Heart 78
*Poem No. 2444* 81
Heart of the Truth 83
*Poem No. 1377* 86
House of Love 88
*Poem No. 332* 91
Divine Pearl 94
*Poem No. 1390* 96
Flow of Life 98
*Poem No. 782* 101
Finding the Path 105
*Poem No. 563* 109

Beyond the Body   112
*Poem No. 215*   115
Spiritual Ecstasy   118
*Poem No. 2309*   121
The Winegiver   124
*Poem No. 1382*   126
Madness of Love   128
*Poem No. 2131*   131
Beyond Consciousness   134
*Poem No. 323*   137
Thought and Rationality   139
*Poem No. 1122*   142
Path of Glory   144
*Poem No. 638*   148
Traveling Beyond   151
*Poem No. 214*   154
Song of Freedom   156
*Poem No. 1710*   158
Dance of Freedom   161
*Poem No. 1554*   163
House of Ruin   166
*Tarji-band No. 25*   169
Pinnacle of Creation   171
*Poem No. 2840*   174
Essence of Love   177
*Poem No. 1770*   180
Purity of Love   182
*Poem No. 2501*   185
Union with the Source   187
*Poem No. 898*   190
Sweetness of Bliss   193
*Poem No. 1987*   196
Comfort of the Soul   198
*Poem No. 207*   200
Mystery of the Essence   202
*Poem No. 1458*   205
Joy of Eternal Love   208
*Poem No. 1395*   210

Connecting with the Soul     213
    *Poem No. 945*     216
    Soul of the Soul     218
    *Poem No. 1805*     221
    Ultimate Reality     223
    *Poem No. 1*     225
    Spiritual Redeemers     227
    *Poem No. 2277*     230
    *Breaking the Lock*     232
    *Poem No. 1375*     235
    Gift of Love     238
    *Poem No. 322*     241
    Silence of Love     243
    *Poem No. 2219*     247

Quoted Mystics and Sufi Masters     249

About the Author     256

# PREFACE

Many books have been written about Rumi and about his life and ideology. He has been called a spiritual leader, a philosopher, a mystic and a poet. Any single one of these descriptions is only the tip of a wave in the fathomless ocean that is Rumi.

Throughout recorded history, the name Jalal Uddin Rumi has been synonymous with love. Rumi's love is more than something a person feels; it is a way of life, a sacred path and a profound journey. He shares the experiences of joy and the ecstasy of longing and union, and the grief of separation. His poetic images and expressions are totally unique. They overflow from the fullness and depths of his heart. To be able to read Rumi's poetry, one needs to step outside the intellect and let the heart lead the way to fully experience and feel the deeper meaning in his poetic words.

*Expression is a blight in the flow of feeling.* \*

Within the past three decades, the name Rumi has been synonymous with poetry in the western world. Rumi has been presented as a poet mainly because his divine words have been interpreted and shared by accomplished poets. They have introduced him to prepare the way for the revelation of the true divinity of his being. In his own words, he says he has waited hundreds of years to speak his truth.

The purpose of this book is to reveal the deeper identity of Rumi, not just as a poet in the way we have come to know him in the west. This book is titled, *Rumi Revealed*, because the intention of it is to reveal the true essence of the divine words that have come through Rumi. The chapters are designed to present the concepts hidden within his words and to give readers a chance to study and reflect on them. In addition, it presents the voices of the mystics who came before Rumi and after him, to allow them to speak and affirm the richness of his profound revelations.

The divine concepts of Rumi flow through those connected with their spiritual hearts. Rumi was one who fell in love with an earthly human being and his amazing journey launched him to the height of divinity.

Rumi has left extremely valuable footprints for us to follow. The path he offers to us opens a unique and magnificent portal to love. There is a divine purpose revealed in these revelations, which guides us to expand and elevate through love. They deepen our understanding and allow us to experience the kind of transformation that would help us become divine love for all humanity.

The *Divan of Shams* was written in an ecstatic state as Rumi danced and played the sitar and sang what was being revealed within him. The golden truth is concealed in the original languages and the complexity of language that he uses, all which require an intense focus and great care in translating his words. He shares his concepts through his use of metaphor, his use of multiple languages and by choosing words with many possible meanings. He does this in order to protect and preserve the pearls of wisdom hidden beneath the dust of the stars and in the golden light of the sun. Rumi has been waiting for a very long time to reveal his deepest insights to us.

My personal encounter with Rumi's poetry started when I was a pre-school child. My uncle, a Sufi mystic, was the one who introduced me to Rumi, even before I was able to read or write. It was also my uncle who encouraged me to develop my artistic ability through painting while meditating on concepts of mystics. Throughout my artistic career, many of Rumi's verses, as well as the work of other mystics, have inspired my paintings. In the beginning, I used to randomly pick a verse, read it thoroughly and meditate on it for a while. As images developed within me, I would dip my brush in paint and let the colors take their course across the canvas. It felt very familiar to me, almost as if Rumi or another mystic had already painted a similar image or feeling with words in their poetry.

Now when I paint, I am not envisioning a particular poem. As I discover certain images on my canvas, I recall a particular verse or a specific mystical concept. As I begin to paint, I feel a certain energy that is now moving through me has been with Rumi in another time.

During the past decade, while teaching my artistic technique, painting with spirit, many of the students, who heard me talk about the approach of the mystics to life and creativity, encouraged me to conduct classes and seminars on the poetry of Rumi. Those classes were held at the University of

Transformational Studies and Leadership in Southern California. Some of the ideas for the text of this book have been drawn from the live recordings and insights from those sessions.

Although I was brought up in an environment where the poetry of Rumi and Hafiz were my nursery rhymes, and even though I have studied the works of mystics for over fifty years, translating poems from such a monumental book as the *Divan of Shams* has been a great challenge.

The poetry of the *Divan of Shams* came to Rumi when he was in an ecstatic state. As a result, it is especially difficult to translate these verses through the rational mind. Even after so many years of experiencing and studying Rumi, every time I read one of his poems, I continue to find myself in a different dimension in which I become mindless, and yet, I am completely conscious through a mystical awareness. It is from that deeper dimension that I received the poetry in this book and translated their hidden meanings, as I worked and reworked the verses. I have tried to surrender to the deeper concepts of the poems and let the experience of love guide the translations.

The poetic language of this book has been developed with the literary assistance of Naomi Stone, a writer and poet, who lives in the Midwest. She is also a mystic and a lover of Rumi, whom I have never met in person. Naomi and I created a system of communication to develop the poetic translations, working on the telephone, sending the results back and forth through email, reworking and refining the verses. This process continued until I would be satisfied that the result was the closest possible version of the original Farsi verse, and Naomi would be satisfied with the poetic language in English.

**I do not claim this book to be a scholarly study of Rumi. I believe that anyone attempting to analyze Rumi from a philosophical perspective or even from a poetic framework would not be recognizing the creative power continuing to unfold in his verses. In Rumi's own words:**

*It is not possible to fit the ocean into a pitcher!*

A difficulty in translating the poetry of Rumi is that much of the terminology used in the *Divan of Shams* is delivered through metaphors that cannot be found in a regular dictionary. To illuminate that, I have included some of the essential mystical expressions used by Rumi and other prominent mystics of the time as they pertain to each specific poem. I have also included certain Sufi phrases and expressions in the text to expand the particular images used.

The potency and the depth of the subjects covered in the *Divan of Shams* is far greater than any introduction could ever describe or explain. The concepts included here are to allow the experiences of the early mystics who have felt that brush with the divine. They are to light the way to the poems and to help to open some of the profound meaning in the messages of Rumi.

My hope is that this book could be read in the same manner that it has been written. I am probing deeply into the hidden metaphors to discover new possibilities and meanings. Perhaps we can discover our power as human beings in a similar way that the divine words flowed through Rumi. We can read his poetry without the use of intellect or our analytical minds. We can read Rumi in the spirit of love.

**One can never assume that anyone can fully understand Rumi. Yet, it is possible to reveal a new dimension by searching the deeper concepts of his work through the heart.**

Hopefully, the world will one day learn more about the absolute wonder of Molana Jalal Uddin Rumi. I trust that the many translations and interpretations will help add insight to reveal the true gift that his poetry of love is to the world.

---

\* Throughout the book, I have quoted lines or verses from the poetry of Rumi from the *Divan of Shams,* as well as the Masnavi, to illustrate an idea in the introduction to each poem. I have identified the poetry of the *Divan of Shams* by putting it in italics whenever it is quoted or presented as a complete poem by Rumi.

# Introduction

*Footprints lead to the shore of the sea!*
*Beyond that point,*
*no trace remains.*

Molana Jalal Uddin Rumi

Among a great body of poetry, letters and discourses, that reflect Rumi's concepts and ideas, two books stand out. One is the *Masnavi*, his better known work, considered by many scholars to be a book on an equal level to a scripture. The *Masnavi* was originally introduced to English speaking readers by R. A. Nicholson (1868–1945) through his complete translations and commentaries. Much of Rumi's poems that have been published in English within the past two decades are basically poetic versions of Nicholson's translations of the *Masnavi*.

Rumi's other celebrated work is a large collection of love sonnets called the *Divan of Shams\**, also known as *Divan e Kabir*, the Great Divan. It is an astounding collection of 44,282 verses that are said to have poured from Rumi in a condition that could only be defined as pure ecstasy and an annihilation of the worldly self.

*Among the thousands of I's and we's,*
*see what a wonderful I, I am!*
*Listen to my cries!*
*Don't cover my mouth!*

*Now that I am out of control,*
*don't obstruct my path,*
*for I'll stomp and smash*
*whatever's in my way!*

The complete *Divan of Shams* is considerably new even in Persian literature. The most reliable edition was done by an Iranian scholar of Rumi, Badi`uzzamân Forôzânfar, published in Tehran in 1957 and enlarged in 1962. I did not have the opportunity to attend any of the late Professor Forôzânfar's classes or lectures. Fortunately, I did have the chance to be exposed to a deeper level of the poetry of the *Divan of Shams* through one of his most qualified students, Professor Shahparaki, with whom I studied Rumi intensely for a period of six years. The poetry selected for this book is a medley from the *Divan of Shams* that I have translated directly from the Persian manuscript of Forôzânfar's edition.

My intention has been not to drop or eliminate any line from the verses simply because I might lack an understanding of the words that were used eight centuries ago in Farsi. To reach the depth of the poetry, and to find suitable English words to reflect Rumi's concepts properly, certain poems or verses have taken long periods of research and reflection.

**The poetry that is gathered in the *Divan of Shams* began sometime after Rumi met Shams of Tabriz. It was Shams' persuasive spiritual supremacy that took Rumi out of his rational world into the madness of love and opened his eyes to many of the bewildering secrets of the universe. It is through this dimension of exaltation that Rumi's poetry seems to have evolved in the *Divan*.**

According to the available evidence, it was the sudden departure of Shams from Konya that originated the outpouring of ecstatic poetry through Rumi. Many scholars believe that when Rumi was convinced he would not find his spiritual beloved again, he created the essence of Shams within himself to reflect the poetic verses.

The given title is *Divan of Shams* instead of *Divan of Rumi*. Giving a different person's name to the *Divan* rather than the customary use of the poet's name is the result of Rumi's annihilation of self in his love for Shams. Rumi considered his own poetry as the work of Shams, thus finishing many of his *ghazals* (sonnets) with the name of Shams, instead of the customary tradition of including one's own name. At other times, he used the concept of "silence" to mean the transcendence of mind.

**What has made the *Divan of Shams* stand out among so many other books about love is the transcendence of Rumi's mystical love for Shams into a divine love, or into the love for a perfect human being.**

Rumi did not set out with the intention of saving the poems or to create a collection of poetry. The poems seem to pour from the mouth of a person who is in a deep dream rather than concentrated attention.

It is evident that, in most cases, Rumi was not even conscious of the fact that these were poems. At times, even the rhythm and rhyming sounds of his poetry feel as if they come after the fact, following behind his concepts and images. Sometimes, we find words that are out of place and outside the accepted standards, such as the unusual use of a metaphor, and occasionally, even crude words, which one would not expect from such an established scholarly figure. It is here we can see that Rumi was not concerned with the limitations of the physical world or language in his poetry.

Rumi maintained a constant flow of words, removed from any constraint or framework. He allowed his imagination to roam freely within the spiritual realm in any direction. Whenever he felt an affiliation with a certain word, new concepts and ideas started to develop. Sometimes, Rumi would use a word from a different language to better explain his idea. One thought would flow into another, and one wave of ecstatic narrative would lead to another, even before the first one was completed!

Rumi did not have to be in any particular condition, place, or time to deliver his poetry; it was spontaneously flowing through him. Day or night, he could be walking, dancing, sitting at home, on a street, in a bazaar, in the bathhouse, or in a mosque, and the verses just kept flowing continuously.

His followers and devotees, especially his older son, Sultan Valad, who was almost always in the presence of his father, wrote down the poetry. There was no plan, no outline, or particular order that was ever developed. The verses were written down as they were being said or sung. No titles were given to the poems. The titles that we find in English versions of Rumi's poetry are attributed to subsequent translations.

In the *Divan of Shams*, Rumi is not bound by any limitation or structure. His horizons extend from the infinite to the infinite. He shows no interest in petty, mundane, or mediocre concerns. He sees the physical world and the invisible world as one unit, and he considers the purpose of existence to be for the human being to experience the Self between these two worlds.

*The world is like the water in a stream;*
*it seems limited, yet it constantly renews itself.*

***Since beyond what we see, the world has no limits;***
***where does the new come from, and***
***where does the old go?***

Rumi sees life as the union of the two opposites. The world and the soul of the world are not separate from each other. Rumi sees existence as the fusion of the two worlds. God is in both worlds, and the Union is the result of these two worlds coming together. The new is constantly being born as the two connect. The human being has free will and is able to feel the physical world and the soul of the world at the same time.

Rumi believes that love is the power that moves creation as a whole. It is flowing through every particle of existence and brings them in ecstasy, whirling to connect to each other. Life without love is not even possible. The measure of the quality of life is the numbers of experiences that relate to love.

**The poetry of the *Divan of Shams* helps us to transcend from physical love to divine love. It moves us from philosophical theories to ecstatic drunkenness and to self-annihilation.**

Rumi does not consider himself either a philosopher or a poet. In fact, he makes fun of both in his verses. He sees logical thinking as an enemy and poetic structure as a limiting framework for love. Yet, his ecstatic drunkenness offers us some of the most valuable philosophical discussions and the greatest love poems of all times. He does not accept the validity of reason, and yet he offers reasons for the existence of the universe, for God, for the soul, and for life outside of our physical dimension.

Rumi's love of nature is very apparent in the *Divan of Shams*. He speaks of the wind, of the earth, water and fire, the ant and elephant, the seed and soil, and the beauty of nature throughout his works. To him, nature is the reflection of God. He describes the human journey in the following verses:

> *I died as mineral and became a plant.*
> *I died as plant and rose to animal.*
> *I died as animal, and I became human.*
> *Why should I fear anything?*
> *When was I ever less by dying?*

Rumi places mankind above everything else in creation.

> *From the limits of the soil to the human being,*
> *there are thousands of levels.*
> *I have taken you from place to place,*
> *never to leave you along the way.*

Life is a progression and not the perfection of a fixed absolute. Sometimes, he describes such theories with the conviction of a philosopher; while at other times, he expresses them with the thrill of a romantic poet. He takes mankind to the highest level and sees us transcending the angels.

> *In the school of humanity,*
> *when you become intimate with God,*
> *you reside on the king's throne*
> *and teach the angels the nature of the divine.*

Rumi's annihilation in the divine fills him with pure love for the creator and for all that is created. His poetry gives us a taste of union with divine. He describes the discovery and the sensation of being melted in love and tells us how to become empty of the self, like the reed flute, to be available to receive the divine breath.

The poetry of the *Divan of Shams* rushes along like a strong flood that takes with it any new idea or thought that appears along its course. Throughout the *Divan*, the reader feels as if the poems are coming from a source that is completely selfless and dissolved in love. It is the lack of logical attention that makes the poetry of the *Divan* feel like a powerful energy that whirls together reason, honor, justice, and faith and dissolves them all into the divine sea of love.

A question I am often asked is, why has Rumi suddenly reappeared after almost eight centuries? The answer is that he never disappeared. The merging of the east and the west through recent globalization, and the introduction of the Internet, has given the west access to a broader awareness of the various cultures and philosophies of the east.

Expanding interest in spiritual realms has drawn people to Rumi's depth of understanding of the nature of mankind and to his ability to build a bridge between the physical and the spiritual worlds. He does this by encompassing our religious beliefs within a more universal possibility of freedom, revealing how all find their connection in Love.

**Rumi's concepts and ideas are timeless, and that is one of the main reasons that he is freely accepted in today's world. He does not associate himself with any place or geographic location, for he feels that he evolves from the soul of his beloved. Love creates him, and it frees him to communicate with everyone beyond the limits of time and place.**

Rumi is also known as the founder of Molavi, a special sect of Sufi practice. Rumi himself, however, did not belong to any set belief system or ideology, for his religion was one of love, which he considers separate from the formal doctrines of organized or institutional religion. Yet, his path of love is inclusive of all religions in a spiritual context. That is what makes him so different from most other mystics. Rumi is able to put aside all prejudice, rules, sects, and religious framework and place his emphasis on the importance of mankind as the center of all creation.

Like most other humanitarian masters, Rumi teaches us that we can overcome any hostility that separates us from others or from ourselves by recognizing the unlimited power within us, and by using our ability to spread unconditional love.

---

\* The word Divan means a collection of poetry in Farsi.

# RUMI'S LIFE

The personal life of a poet or an artist, in the culture of the east, is not known in such detail as one can find in western literature. Usually, the names are hidden behind the works. The biography of the artists and the poets can be figured out only through various historical events that happened during their lives. Classical painters of the east usually signed their names as 'servant of' or 'devotee of', followed by the name of the dignitary who had commissioned the work.

When it comes to the life of such great mystics and poets as Sana'i, Attar, Saadi or even Hafiz, there is little information for a curious reader to learn about their lives. It is accepted in the east that the best way to know about certain mystics or poets is through in-depth study of their own words.

Rumi is an exception, for not only do we have the account of his contemporaries and near contemporaries, such as Sepahsalar, Aflaki, and his own son, Baha Uddin Valad; we also have his own vivid descriptions in his poetry. The collection of discourses by Shams of Tabriz gives us good insight to form and expand the biography of this great mystic. Rumi, however, did not care about putting himself in such limitation or constraints to have to be concerned about time or place as it related to any event, including describing his own life.

*My life can be summed up in three statements:*
*I was raw;*
*I was cooked,*
*and I was burned.*

What is significant to know about Jalal Uddin Rumi's life is that he was born in 1207 in Balkh in what is today's Afghanistan, which at that time was a part of the Persian Empire. Rumi himself rejected the idea of being from any particular place in the east or in the west. He also disassociated himself from being connected with any formalized religion, which included Zoroastrianism, an ancient religion of Persians, as well as Islam, of which his father was a highly respected theologian.

The Thirteenth Century was one of the darkest times in history. Genghis Khan and his army attacked the Persian Empire, which at the time was the center of culture and prosperity. Artisans, merchants, scholars and poets would migrate from different parts of the known world to benefit from all the opportunities that were available.

The attack of Genghis Khan was unexpected and was treated initially by the rulers of the Persian Empire as unimportant. Within a short period, he was able to capture and destroy town after town without any resistance. As his army moved forward, destruction and massive killings left such fear in the empire that many people fled toward the west to be safe from the intruders. Genghis Khan's army destroyed everything and killed everyone alive. They showed mercy for no one, not even the cats and the dogs. The Mongol army would make hills of dead bodies wherever they moved.

In order to escape the Mongol invasion and destruction, Rumi's father, Baha Uddin, gathered his entire family and many of his followers and started on a journey toward possible safety in the west. The thirteen-year-old Jalal Uddin (later called Rumi) always stayed close to his father as they traveled on foot as well as on horses, camels, and mules across vast deserts, high mountains, and wide rivers. Some died along the way and others survived until they finally settled in Konya in the northwestern provinces of the Seljuk Empire, presently known as Turkey.

What remained with Rumi after the years of this long journey were the never-to-be-forgotten memories of sand storms in the deserts, of the strong current of rivers they had to cross, and the travelers passing by on their way to or from India, China, Saghsin, Iraq or Khorasan. At night, under the stars, discussions were always about heaven and hell, Adam and Eve, and the stories from or related to the Koran. Listening to all of these lofty ideas, the soul of the young Jalal Uddin was already traveling in a different dimension at an early age.

One event that was certainly a formative step toward the development of a new consciousness for the thirteen-year-old Rumi took place in Nishapur. It was there that he met the great Persian mystic poet, Attar, who presented him with a copy of his *Asra'r Nameh*, the *Book of Mysteries*. It is reported that Attar was very impressed by the young man, and he told his father,

Baha Uddin, that his son would one day set the spiritual seekers of the world on fire.

*The Book of Mysteries*, which Attar had written during his own youth, was a divine book to young Rumi and led him to immerse himself in it through the long and tiresome journey. Attar had written this book in the style of rhyming couplets known as *masnavi*. It was Rumi's familiarity with that style of poetry that most likely influenced him to create his own great work of the *Masnavi* near the end of his life.

Aside from the poetic style, Attar's *Book of Mysteries* taught the young Rumi many secrets about the way mystics develop their inner union with the Divine. It revealed to him the essence of true love, which is the deepest concept developed in Rumi and remained permanently with him throughout his life.

> The heart, in the vast ocean of contemplation,
> cannot find anything but bewilderment.
> While going through this phase, the heart becomes
> observant and finds the clues to many mysteries.
> 
> Attar

Rumi's spiritual awareness developed at a very early age. He also developed a scholarly grasp and understanding of the Koran. He was an exceptional child, who was bright, curious, swift, and extremely intelligent. The long and fearful journey through the desert, the dust along the way, the sounds of bells on camels, and the shouts of travelers were his first encounters with the outside world beyond his own physical senses.

Baha Uddin, his family and followers were warmly welcomed in Konya, which by then had become a haven for many Persian immigrants who were anxious to live away from the disastrous massacres of Genghis Khan and his army. Within a short time, Baha Uddin gained a great popularity as a religious scholar and a Sufi. Although Rumi was married and had two sons at an early age, he was often in the presence of his father. Baha Uddin died when Rumi was twenty-four years old.

Upon the death of Baha Uddin, the young Rumi was not quite ready to take over the responsibility of becoming a religious leader, so one of his fathers' disciples, Borhan, took over the position. This created an opportunity for Rumi to move away from Konya to study in Damascus and Aleppo, the two most important centers of Islamic studies during the thirteenth century. After seven years of intense studies, Rumi was unequaled in rational, traditional, and spiritual knowledge. He then returned to Konya to become Borhan's apprentice for the next three years.

Under Borhan's guidance, Rumi undertook a period of living in a hermitage, practicing ascetic exercises, and studying his father's spiritual notebooks and the Koran commentaries. Eventually, Rumi's mastery of the Gnostic path satisfied Borhan that the young man was no longer in need of a mentor or guide, and he was ready to teach and preach in Konya.

For the next four years, Rumi assumed his father's religious teaching position and became a professor of law and a preacher to a community of mystically oriented disciples. He attained great fame during this period and was recognized as an expert in Islamic law. He also achieved certain popularity as a speaker and representative of an authentic and accessible mode of Islamic spirituality. His sermons and discourses attracted a great many disciples, some of whom were merchants and artisans and many from the ruling class. Women also attended his lectures, and a number of them became Rumi's disciples.

A great number of Islamic scholars, who were running away from the oppression and destruction by the Mongols, moved to Konya and became disciples of the young Rumi. He was the guide and master to over four hundred scholars and students and had professorial positions in four different schools at the same time.

If Rumi's life had continued in a similar manner, the world would not have had the opportunity to benefit from the creative expression of the great mystic he eventually became. However, life had been rapidly preparing him for what was yet to come.

In 1244, an extraordinary event occurred that changed Rumi's life profoundly and gave rise to the extraordinary outpouring of some of the greatest love sonnets of all times. The present book includes a small selection of those poems.

The event, which is believed by some, to be one of the most amazing incidents in the development and expansion of human self-awareness, was Rumi's encounter with Shams of Tabriz, a mystic, who was destined to expand Rumi to a dimension far beyond what any ordinary person had been able to reach.

Shams of Tabriz became the representation of the perfect and complete man and the true image of the *Beloved* that Rumi had long been seeking. From the time they met, the ecstatic love of God manifested in Rumi through sublime poetry in a trance state, while playing or listening to devotional music or dancing. In the following poem, he is describing the ecstatic sensation he was feeling within.

*O friends!*
*How can I be identified?*
*I don't know my self.*

*I'm neither a Christian, nor a Jew,*
*neither a Zoroastrian, nor a Moslem.*

*I am not of the east, nor the west,*
*neither of the land nor the sea.*
*I am not from nature's mine,*
*nor from the revolving universe.*

*I am not of dust, nor of water,*
*neither of wind nor of fire.*
*I'm not of the angels, nor of earthlings,*
*not of time, nor of space.*

*I'm not from India, nor from China,*
*neither from Bulgaria, nor from Saghsin.*
*I am neither from the kingdom of Iraq,*
*nor from the land of Khorasan.*

*I am not of this world, nor of the next,*

*not of Heaven, nor of Hell.*
*I am not of Adam, nor of Eve,*
*neither of the Garden of Eden, nor of Paradise.*

*My place is the placeless.*
*My trace is the traceless.*
*I am neither of body, nor of soul,*
*for I am the soul of the Beloved.*

*I have abolished duality from myself.*
*I have seen the two worlds as One!*
*One I seek, One I know,*
*One I see, and One I call.*

*The Beloved is the first and the last.*
*The Beloved is the outward and the inward.*
*I know nothing else but*
*for the Beloved and from the Beloved.*

*Filled with ecstasy from the wine of love,*
*I have passed beyond the two worlds!*
*Except for being a libertine*
*and a drunk, I have no other existence.*

*If I spend a moment in my life without you,*
*I am ashamed for that moment and that life.*

*If I am honored to spend*
*a moment in my life with you,*
*I would put both worlds under my feet*
*and dance forever in joy.*

*O Shams of Tabriz,*
*I am so joyfully drunk in this world,*
*that except for songs of ecstasy and joy,*
*I have nothing else to say.*

Note: The above poem is excluded from Forôzânfar's edition of *Divan of Shams*. It has been translated from Monshi Nool edition printed in India, 1923.

# TRANSFORMATION

The meeting between Rumi and Shams took place on Saturday, November 28, 1244. According to descriptions given by Rumi's disciples, it was mid-morning on a cool autumn day when Rumi came face to face with Shams of Tabriz. At the time, the well-respected thirty-seven year old Islamic scholar was leading his followers through one of Konya's bazaars, when he met a sixty year old wandering dervish, who had recently come to town. His name was Shams, and because he was from Tabriz, a city in northwestern Iran, he was known as *Shams e Tabrizi* or Shams of Tabriz.

> As the two met, Shams asked Rumi,
> **O master, who was greater, Mohammad or Bastami?***
> Without hesitation, Rumi answered,
> **What kind of question is that? Mohammad was always right for he was the Prophet of God; Bastami was only a follower of the Prophet.**
> Shams asked,
> **Then how come Mohammad prayed to God saying he did not acknowledge and worship him as he should, but Bastami said to behold me with pure eyes to observe the greatness of God's glory within me?**
> On hearing these words, the learned Islamic scholar suddenly realized the depth of the question and dismounted to answer the stranger,
> **Bastami had taken one gulp of the divine and stopped there, but for Mohammad the way was always unfolding.**

Immediately after this conversation, Rumi grasped Shams' hand and took him to his house to continue their discussions. From then on, the two spent a great number of hours together everyday. They were continually immersed in spiritual discussions away from all followers and disciples. Within a short time, Rumi was transformed from a religious leader into a free-spirited being, no longer interested in intellectual discussions.

Shams of Tabriz, from the moment that he arrived in Konya, began to have a powerful influence on Rumi. It was only a few weeks after his arrival that Rumi gave up his own position as an Islamic leader and became entirely devoted to Shams. He gave up lecturing, ignored his own disciples, withdrew from everyone and became totally immersed in Shams and his ideology. He spent day after day with Shams and turned against many of the religious conventions that he had previously held.

> *Whether I go east or west,*
> *or fly to the heavens,*
> *there is no sign of life in me,*
> *until I see a sign of you.*

> *I was a devout leader of a country.*
> *I held a pulpit.*
> *Fate made my heart fall in love*
> *and follow you dancing.*

To be in the presence of Shams, Rumi gave up his leadership position and become a person without identity, one who was lost in love. In a way, the mission of Shams was to make a complete transformation in Rumi and to bring him down from his egoistic fame into an ordinary person. This was to prepare him for the change that was to follow. It was through this radical change that Rumi could sacrifice the self in the mystical death of love. He was transformed from a clergyman, who was shedding modest light about him like a candle, into a brilliant light that has never ceased to shine since it was ignited.

Shams remained in the company of Rumi for a period of fourteen months, but the jealousy of Rumi's followers finally became unbearable and influenced him to leave Konya. The departure of Shams was too stressful for Rumi. Finally his followers and relatives who were worried about Rumi's distressed condition, searched for Shams until they found him in Damascus and brought him back. After his return, Shams stayed in Konya for just over a year and he disappeared again. This time, Shams was never to be found. It is speculated that possibly Rumi's followers murdered him.

Rumi personally looked for Shams for month after month and from town to town, until he was finally convinced that Shams was gone forever. Separation from Shams was like separation from God for Rumi. It was after the second disappearance of Shams that Rumi became completely drowned in a state of the ecstasy of longing, and a stream of exalted poetry began to flow from his lips in a litany of love.

> *In the midst of the darkness,*
> *a moon appeared with its brilliance.*
> *Stepping down from the clouds,*
> *it glanced at me.*
>
> *Like a falcon*
> *that hunts a bird and steals it away,*
> *it captured me*
> *and flew back to infinite space.*
>
> *As I looked for myself,*
> *I could not find me,*
> *for my body had become all soul*
> *in the tenderness of love.*
>
> *The nine spheres of heaven*
> *dissolved in that moon*
> *as the ship of my existence*
> *drowned in the sea of love.*

Rumi became more ecstatic in his worship and started to express his love of God through an attitude of self-renunciation, yielding of control, and through his constant ecstasy. Shams of Tabriz had captivated him completely and had transformed his spirituality both externally and internally.

**The way Shams came to Konya looking for Rumi was almost like a self-fulfilling prophecy, something Shams was destined and divinely guided to do.**

The first instruction of Shams to Rumi was to stop his exterior learning, and made him drop all the books that had brought him knowledge into a well. This was an act of madness in itself, as each one of his books was one of a kind in various fields of philosophy, theology, astronomy, law and logic.

In his madness, Rumi began to dance, play and listen to devotional music, which was behavior that he had not previously sanctioned. He could not see himself separated from Shams and was constantly looking for him everywhere. As the poetry of love and longing were pouring out, the verses were written down and collected by several of his disciples including his own son, Sultan Valad. The poetry was primarily in Persian with occasional verses in Arabic, Turkish, and Greek. This is the poetry that was later collected into the *Divan of Shams*.

**Shams of Tabriz was like a doctor curing the illness of Rumi who was popular, arrogant, and untouchable. He was in fact like the Ka'ba, the direction of everyone's worship. Before the meeting with Shams, Rumi's followers would have to stand behind him if they wished to speak with him, and Rumi would not even look at them while he was carrying on the conversation. They would ask a question from behind him, and he would answer it in the air. That is how respected Rumi was before Shams found him and before the two met.**

The spiritual love for Shams remained with Rumi for the rest of his life. It was years later that he developed close friendships with two men including Hessam, who wrote down the *Masnavi* as Rumi dictated it to him in his later years. Molana Jalal Uddin Rumi departed from this world on December 17, 1273.

The poetry of the *Divan of Shams* is a vivid example of how human love begins with earthly desire and attraction and transcends everything as it expands into divine love. It is an undeniable fact that it was Shams of Tabriz who awakened a belief in Rumi that the most valuable gift in life is the presence of the Beloved within.

One major distinction between the mysticism of Rumi in comparison with other mystics is that they generally reveal the humbler side of the mystic, while Rumi always looks at mankind as the pride of the universe, and he places the human being higher than the heaven and the angels. The seeker of truth, or the mystic, is constantly looking for the awareness of his function in this world. As we observe in Rumi, rather than finding a function, his very heart and soul becomes an expression of divine love and a guiding beacon for others.

The whole process of how a master transfers the divine light of love to another is elevated in the expressive stream of consciousness that Rumi shares with humanity as divine poetry that radiates like the sun. To draw near to it is to feel its power. Many have written books about how this process is channeled, but the details are unimportant. When it happens, the lover is immersed in it, like looking out from inside the sun. The lover doesn't see the self, because he has lost it in the beloved or in love.

The following poem is almost like an autobiography of Rumi referring to his own life as it was changed from an ordinary one into an extraordinary life through the power of love that he experienced in his transcendent relationship with Shams of Tabriz.

Rumi is considering Love as the truth that brings eminence and raises consciousness from the earthly plane to higher levels, so that we might be able to experience the exalted life that we were meant to live. As the wayfarer reaches a higher level of consciousness beyond the physical realm, the ordinary life begins to seem limited and confined in a much smaller world. It is somewhat like the joy of living life in an unlimited free space rather than being contained in a prison cell. The world of divine lovers expands to include the whole universe, and it is from that dimension that lovers shine above the seven heavens and receive the assurance of immortal life.

Whatever symbol or metaphor we attract through our longing, divine love comes flowing through it. Divine love can flow through anything, split it open, dissolve it, melt it, and make it bloom, or bring a powerful human being to his knees. In this poem, Rumi's eloquent surrender speaks to the magnificence of it!

---

* Bastami was a Sufi leader and one of the most influential mystics of all times. He is known among the Sufis as the king of the mystics. His ideology was a major influence for Shams of Tabriz, which eventually impacted Rumi. His Sufi doctrine was based on being enraptured by divine love and through annihilation in the Truth. Sufi literature is filled with many anecdotes about Bastami, his discourses and statements. Please refer to the appendix at the end of this book for more information on Bastami.

## DİVAN OF SHAMS: POEM NO. 1393

*I was dead; I became alive.*
*I was tears; I became laughter.*
*The power of love arrived*
*and made me everlasting power!*

*I have seen everything.*
*I have no fear.*
*I have the heart of a lion!*
*I shine like Venus.*

*Love told me I am not mad;*
*I am not fit for this house.*
*I am mad!*
*I am just a ring in your chain.*

*Love told me I am not drunk,*
*that I should get out of this shackle.*
*I am drunk, look at me!*
*I am overflowing with joy.*

*Love told me I am not dead,*
*that I am not drowned in joy.*
*Before love's resurrecting gaze,*
*I fell to nothing, and I died!*

*Love told me I am a clever little man*
*filled with ego and doubt.*
*I am not clever.*
*I am a fool, a bewildered fool!*
*I am neither here nor there.*

*Love told me I am a candle,*
*that I am the Kiblah of this crowd.*
*I am not a candle; I have no crowd.*
*I am scattered like smoke.*

Love told me I am a sheikh,
that I am a leader, and I am a guide!
I am not a sheikh; I am not a leader.
I am here at your command.

Love told me I have wings and feathers,
and would not grant me wings!
In the fire of desire for love,
I lost my wings and feathers.

The new power told me not to worry,
I don't need to move!
The grace and generosity
of love is mine!

The past attachments would not fall away.
They screamed that they still were mine!
I yielded and did not move.
I am now still and grounded.

You are the fountain of the sun.
I am the shadow of the willow.
As you shine on me,
I melt and die in my self.

My heart felt the glow of life
ripped open in bloom.
I was dressed in a new veil,
and dropped the old ragged one.

Filled with ecstasy at dawn,
the new veil shone with pride.
I used to be slave to a mule.
I am now king and a lord!

The new paper wrap
is grateful to love's endless sugar,
for sweetness filled me

*making me one with love.*

*This dark and enraged dust
is grateful to heaven's wheel,
for through its graceful turn,
I have become the receiver of light.*

*The wheel of heaven is grateful
to the king, the kingdom, and the angel,
for through divine grace
I have become the giver of light.*

*The wayfarer of truth
is grateful for love's eminence;
I have become a shining star
beyond the seven heavens!*

*I was Venus, now I am the moon;
I am a celestial wheel with countless turns!
I was Joseph,
now I am the creator of Joseph.*

*I am yours, O eminent moon;
gaze into me and into your self,
for through the trace of your smile,
I am a rose garden in eternal bloom.*

*Like a chess piece,
I am silent, yet expressive,
for I am a blissful rook
castling with the king of the world.*

# POWER OF LOVE

Love is the power of creation and the ultimate gift of life. It purifies the soul from corporal contamination and eliminates the self-seeking passion or lust that could lead to evil actions.

Love is a continual flow of desire and attraction that moves through the heart. Love is about joy and freedom. It goes beyond a merely physical attraction and explores the infinite power that is hidden within its essence and purity. If the flow is directed toward a certain beloved, the energy of love is transformed to more exclusive feelings.

*Love is an endless sea.*
*Love is divine madness.*
*Love is the source of light.*
*Love is the expression of the heart.*

Love is the alchemy of life and the foundation of everything that exists in the world. The flow of love is the catalyst for the movement of all life. Even the rotation of the galaxies is a form of the expression of love.

*Love begins with*
*the realization of equality in relationship*
*and leads to its fulfilment.*
*Through attraction, we reach love.*
*Through love, we gain balance.*
*The power of love transforms*
*the mountain into the sea.*
Attar

When fully dissolved in love, a person loses the awareness of time and space and burns with desire for the union with the beloved. Experiencing the ecstasy of love is to lose all sense of existing separately from the beloved. When the feeling of oneness is fully developed, the lover is in true love.

*Love brings the sea into boiling*
*and turns the mountain into a pebble.*

> *Love creates infinite openings*
> *in the dark sky and shudders*
> *the earth with its magnitude.*
> *If pure love were not infinite,*
> *the universe would cease to exist.*

Inside everyone's heart, there is a garden of life constantly growing and developing, which is the spirit of a person. Love radiates the light of joy upon this spiritual garden in much the same way as the sun shines on a physical garden. When the garden of the heart is brightened with true love, the lover feels an unlimited power and an ever-expanding creative energy within the self.

> *Plant the tree of love,*
> *for it bears the fruit that feeds the heart.*
> *Uproot the hostile sapling,*
> *for it brings suffering to the soul.*
> Hafiz

Through the cherishing and nurturing of love, the heart blooms and opens into the flowering of the soul that offers the beauty and power of true joy. When the soul is filled with joy, the essence of creativity begins to manifest, and the lover becomes a witness to a constant flow of an extraordinary creative power. What will usually interfere with the growth of this truly pure and creative power is allowing the negative and critical thoughts of the mind to dominate, for they become like weeds in a neglected garden. The garden of the heart begins to decay when the ego-self becomes the center of the focus of success.

> *Love burns the self of the lover*
> *with every breath.*
> *When the state is ruined,*
> *it is freed from all burdens.*
> *The nation of love has a different religion.*
> *Love is the nation, the religion, and God.*
> Rumi's Masnavi

Love, in mystical poetry, has two distinct descriptive qualities: worldly love and divine love. Worldly love begins with physical attraction, expands to desire, and flows to a deep longing, culminating in the expression of love. Divine love is the attraction of the soul, the inspiration of joy, and the embrace of the divine essence. True love is divine love, for it offers an increasingly heightened ecstasy, flowing through the union of the lover and the beloved.

Once divine love and its feeling of limitlessness and expansive capacity is experienced, the lover will no longer be satisfied with accepting worldly affection, which is only a fraction of true love. When a person becomes aware of the possibility of becoming as infinite as an ocean, why would anyone want to be only a drop? The acceptance of limits comes from the restraint of the mind blindly seeking status, power, fame and fortune.

The human being has been created to experience the divine nature. However, there are seductive passions and goals that can ultimately limit spiritual growth. Only those who are freed from the goals that limit them, whose hearts are filled with love, discover the opportunity to move forward to claim the divine nature from which they came.

# DİVAN OF SHAMS: POEM NO. 1374

O lovers! O lovers!
I turn the dust into jewels!
O minstrels! O minstrels!
I fill your tambourine with gold!

O thirsty ones! O thirsty ones!
I quench your thirst today.
I turn this earthly dustbin
into a fountain in paradise.
O lonely ones! O lonely ones!
Solution is here! Decree has arrived!
I turn everyone tired of gloom
into a sultan, into a king.

O alchemy! O alchemy! Look into me!
I turn hundreds of
taverns into mosques
and hundreds of gallows into pulpits.

O nonbelievers! O nonbelievers!
I unlock your vision!
I decide who to make a believer,
and who to make a skeptic.

O mouth full of empty words!
You are like wax in the palm of my hands.
If you are a dagger, I turn you into a chalice,
If you are a chalice, I turn you into a dagger.

From sperm you turned into blood
and you grew to become such an elegant being.
Come to me, O heir of Adam!
I will make you ever more graceful!

*I turn sadness into joy!*
*I turn lost into found!*
*I turn wolf into Joseph!*
*I turn bitterness into sweetness!*

*O mouth open to receive!*
*My mouth is open to give.*
*I place every dry lip*
*on the lip of the chalice.*

*O rose picker! O rose picker!*
*Pick a rose from my garden*
*for I turn every shrub*
*into morning glory.*

*O Garden of Heaven! You become*
*more bewildered than the wild poppies,*
*for I turn the dust into jasmine*
*and thorn into roses.*

*O divine wisdom! O divine wisdom!*
*Whatever you command is right!*
*You are the ruler; you are the judge!*
*I become silent and say no more!*

# DIVINE LOVE

The love of Christ is considered divine love realized here on earth. Rumi's love is human love transcending the earth and becoming divine love. It is a love that even if not perfect, always has a spiritual aspect, because the beloved becomes supreme. In both conditions, love is the infinite flow of prosperity.

> *Any physical loss*
> *in the way of love, is a privilege*
> *for it transcends love*
> *from corporal to divine.*

Divine love is the desire of the heart to journey along the path of longing and ecstasy toward intimacy with the Beloved without any limitation. The heart in total surrender guides the journey, for it intuitively knows the way and is aware of the secrets not known to the human mind. The heart is conscious of the deeper mysteries through an inner knowing and familiarity with the power of the soul.

> **O dervish! Unless a person has fallen deeply in love, he is not purified of corporal attachments; unless he is truly pure, he cannot reach the source of purity. When a person falls in love with a limited beloved, he will remain impure and will not be cleansed, for he has stopped the flow of love by not allowing it to expand.**
>
> **The heart that is only partially surrendered to love will always be at a crossroad trying to find the way to the source of purity. While in such a state, that heart is not fully capable for physical, spiritual, or divine expression.**
>
> Al Jili

Expansiveness of love is what exalts a person from the limitations felt in life to the joy of freedom. Recognition of the limitlessness of love is the divine revelation of the created becoming fully conscious of oneness with the creator. Rumi sees limitation in a human being the same as being asleep or dead to the fullness of life. The way to freedom from limitation is to be fully aware that our true identity is discovered in our divine nature, which is the gift of the soul.

The one who is excessively attached to earthly lust and passion is drawn by gravity toward what Rumi calls the 'mud-bed'. Meanwhile, the soul is longing to return to its original source, which is found in divine intimacy. To respond to the call of the heart for divine intimacy is to transcend beyond the mortal love for a particular person, and move beyond all possessions and personal prestige. Pure Love is to focus toward a creative power that is not bound by limitation.

Rumi feels that true joyfulness is free expression of divine play. Logic or rationality has very little or no effect in this state of being. In order to draw the spirit toward the original Soul, love tears down whatever reason attempts to build up. As divine play becomes more spontaneous and free, we feel the joyfulness.

The practice of worship of God by the Sufis is to recognize that everything in existence is connected with God. This is a direct way of reaching God without going through the difficult practices required by most religious belief systems. The idea behind this concept is that when a person comes to the realization that everything is connected with God, he becomes a being of Love. Such a person will have love for everything and everyone without exclusion. He merges with the Beloved, for he has taken on the characteristics and image of God.

Everyone, regardless of their religious belief, can open to developing divine love. The practice is to be open to receive it anywhere at any time without effort. As love begins to radiate from those who do this, they will receive more love from others, which expands the joy within them and for everyone else. This becomes the way to develop an understanding of the true nature of the self in relation to one's environment. This is the deeper meaning of the idea that *man is created in the image of God* as expressed in scripture. The entire universe is created through divine substance that is infinite love, and we are a part of it.

We are made of divine light. The image of God is always shining within us. This indicates that all physical life is made of divine light, carrying divine intelligence and power. We exist on earth to make proper use of it. Recognition of this truth is what helps to develop a more inclusive love for all that has been created. Everything is made of divine substance. We are given the power of imagination and creativity to use divine light for the benefit of all creation, not to personalize it to satisfy the ego-self.

**To a mystic, worshiping God is to learn to love everything and everyone as a part of creation, which is an expression and manifestation of God's infinite love for all.**

Divine love is to have affection and compassion even for those who are different from us, for they are also created in the image of God. By realizing it is the divine power that creates variety for life, we come to accept the practice of divine love and light beyond judgment. Divine love is to learn to love even our enemies, for they are also striving to realize unity with God. Every soul is reaching for the Beloved. Since the Beloved of all is one, there is no separation in any way.

> **Love is the necessary provision for the path of every seeker. Even if you do not feel the love for the divine creator, open to developing love for all that has been created, so you would reach a deeper spiritual level of growth.**
>
> Eyn al Ghozat

Divine love is the power that dissolves opposition and hatred. Any joy we offer to others, we also give to ourselves. Any pain we cause to others, we also suffer ourselves. Since the entire creation is in total balance, when we focus our attention on what we love and not on what we dislike or hate, we are allowing our love to expand to become divine.

As we develop divine love, we realize that life's problems begin to diminish. If not, it is because we simply have not perceived solutions contained within the problems themselves. If the solution is not found, it is often because we are too attached to the opinion or the behavior that originally caused the problem. Divine Love continues to attract us to move toward total surrender of all resistance to its creative power.

# DIVAN OF SHAMS: POEM NO. 2138

O Love!
Is it you bringing us harmony,
or is it the rose gardens
and apple orchards in you?

O bright moon!
Spin and revolve
and scatter your gleaming light
upon all who seek refuge in you!

The taste of bitterness
becomes sweetness in you!
The searching in the dark
finds the light of faith revealed in you!
You transform thistles into jasmine.
Many hearts yield
and surrender to the glory in you!

You have layered heaven,
and you have gifted us
with wings to soar into its mystery.
You transform our every thought
into a desire of the heart!
Everyone is gloriously bewildered in you!

O Love!
How divine is your luring!
Beauty flows from your unseen face!
Your very nature is radiant with joy!
The thrill of every union
is revealed in you!

You manifest vibrant hues in every flower!
Your touch dazzles all creation!
Every particle is attracted to you,
longing to unite

and dwell in you!

Even the excitement of the market
wilts away without your presence!
The vineyards and the meadows wither
without the rain of compassion in you!

Every tree in the garden learns
its dance from you!
Every branch sways
and moves to your rhythm!
The leaf and the fruit are drunk
from the life-giving water flowing in you!

If the garden longs for
the gift of eternal spring,
it is to yield its blossoms
to the divine breeze
from one breath in you!

Among all stars and planets,
it would bring shame
to any star spinning away
from the radiance in you!

How glorious is the laughter
in the garden of your delight!
In the place of a feast,
the soul, as your guest,
savors the delight in you!

I have tried to resist many times before,
and I know there is no joy without you!
There is no ecstasy without
uniting in sweet embrace in you!

I went on a journey and returned!
I traveled from the end to the beginning.

*In my dream,
I see my soul forever grazing
in the splendor of the golden fields in you!*

*Every meadow is a playground
for those who swirl and sway in your love!
Even virgins give birth to new life
in the divine kingdom in you!*

*Every direction leads me nowhere!
Your love has broken every link.
You draw my wayward soul
to the harbor of the Soul in you!*

*The enduring mountain
is humbled in your patience.
The heart is fearless to leap
into the veranda sheltered in you!*

*You have made infinite openings in stones,
metals and mountains
and made the heart like an ant
looking for a way into
plates and fingers in you!*

*If I count until the end of time,
I would still fall short of describing your grace.
How can anyone measure with a cup
the sea of enchantment in you?*

# LONGING FOR LOVE

Longing is usually associated with a condition of missing something or someone. It is not considered a desirable state by those who are interested only in instant satisfaction and indulgence in life.

Longing for love is the description of the condition of the lover who feels separated from the beloved. It is a stream of energy that flows from the heart of the lover reaching for the beloved. This energy takes many forms and goes in many directions as the longing develops. Sometimes, it causes the lover to feel weak; other times it appears as an unlimited power. Sometimes it brings sadness; other times it brings joy.

To the mystics, longing is a powerful energy that moves life toward a deeper experience of love. It is an infinite power that exalts and elevates the lover as it flows through the heart. Longing is like a spiral that expands and contracts the flow of love in much the same way as the rhythm of life does in the cycle of breathing.

> O heart! Behold what longing
> does for every true lover!
> Lightning strikes at midnight
> from the kingdom of the beloved, *Leila*.
> See how the flame of love razes
> the harvest of *Majnun*, the faithful lover!
> Hafiz

Falling deeply in love happens when the lover is able to release all attachments and move beyond bodily passion or physical desire. As the feeling of being separated from the beloved increases, the lover begins to surrender to the strengthening energy of the flow of love. Surrendering to love allows the longing to deepen and consequently, it expands love. Should the beloved emerge to the lover, longing diminishes and so does surrendering.

When the lover feels the acceleration of the movement of life and the deepening intimacy of love through longing, the pain of yearning becomes a source of joy and the absence of causes anguish. The power of love is contrary to any logical or mental description that tries to explain the creative effect of longing. The mysterious touch of the divine is what forms and creates a connection with the human heart.

> A moment of longing is more blissful
> than all the pleasures of the world.
> How can I be cured of love,
> when I am constantly praying
> for the pain of longing?
> — Attar

The expression of love takes place in three phases: longing, union, and satisfaction. Longing intensifies love and makes it more powerful, while satisfaction reduces the fire of love and makes it frail. When we are fully satisfied, we can feel the beginning of the weakening of love. Longing for love develops a strengthening power that can shatter any resistance. It is a phenomenon not fully grasped or understood with rational mind.

> The way of love goes beyond
> mere endurance and satisfaction.
> Come join the circle of lovers.
> Drink the cup of longing with us.
> — Hafiz

The lover experiences the deepest intimacy through the acute longing for the beloved, for the longing opens the heart and purifies it. It creates a protection that prevents the infiltration of any worldly desire or lust for self-satisfaction. Love flows more freely in response, and it becomes even more intensified and unguarded in that freedom.

> *When my yearning is measured and minute,*
> *I am filled with sadness.*
> *When I am wildly longing for you,*
> *I am filled with grace.*

The physical expressions of love are pleasing and satisfying and they are given for our pleasure, but they are only the entry to something much more magnificent. It is human nature to long for more in the mystery of love, for the truth of the beloved is found only through the longing heart. As the mystery of the beloved is unveiled, its expression continues to attract the lover and becomes an invitation for an even greater expansion of love. Mystery becomes the stimulus for the development of the mind to fearlessly move toward the unknown.

Mystery harbors the divine attraction that offers true comfort of the soul and invites unhindered creativity. The experience of being attracted beyond the comfort zone develops an impulse to expand and to discover and create a new realm and level of comfort. It produces a feeling of being more alive, and life becomes more exhilarating.

> **Feel the truth as love proclaims in joy**
> **that we have yielded to endless longing.**
> **Let blessing and kindness**
> **be what others seek.**
> Eyn al Ghozat

The luring and the consent of the beloved in an encouraging and charming way stops the expansion of the ego-self of the lover and nurtures the true expression of the heart.

As the ego-self of the lover is replaced by love alone, the desire to escape from all social amenities expands, and the lover seeks the solitude apart from a common or ordinary life. Everything becomes an invitation to flow in love. The lover welcomes that which expands his longing, even the rejection of the beloved and the reprimands of love.

> *Attraction is the entry to existence!*
> *Let this sweet truth*
> *always be in your heart.*

In the following poem, Rumi reflects how his longing for Shams of Tabriz exalts him from the human realm and becomes the movement and the essence of his transcendent love. The poem reveals that Rumi's desire for the company of Shams is an invitation to move him beyond all images and metaphors toward a reverent silence and pure being of divine presence.

**When it comes to divine love, there is no fullness of satisfaction, for longing continues to increase until it becomes the pain of separation, which is relieved only through divine union.**

As the lover feels closer to reaching divine union, he becomes a powerful witness to the glory of divine love and forgets about the union itself. The lover's entire being is surrendered to the Beloved, and the awareness of the self is gone. This is how mystics describe the transcendence of love through surrendering.

When Shams of Tabriz arrived at Konya for the first time, he did not make any connection with ordinary Sufis.

He said:
**In this world, I have no business with the ordinary. I have not come for them. I'm here to place my thumb over the vein of the leaders to stop the flow of the egoistic mind.**

In fact, this is how he transformed Rumi. In a way, Shams' mission was to bring Rumi down from his egoistic fame and to guide him to become a special human being flowing to divine love. This all happened after Shams departed from Rumi, leaving him with the ever-increasing pain of longing.

It was Rumi's deepest longings for Shams that exalted him beyond the sun and the stars to touch the divine mystery. He found his oneness with the essence of the divine and let it express through him, and the songs continue to be heard and felt. In the poem, he expresses the flow of love through his endless longings.

# DIVAN OF SHAMS: POEM NO. 441

*Show your face,*
*for gardens and roses are what I am longing for!*
*Open your lips,*
*for abundant sweetness is what I am longing for!*

*O glorious sun!*
*Come out of the clouds for a moment!*
*The radiance of your shimmering face*
*is what I am longing for!*

*I heard the drumbeat*
*from your kingdom calling the royal falcon.*
*I have returned!*
*The arm of the Sultan is what I am longing for!*

*Enticingly, you said,*
*Go away and hurt me no more!*
*Your saying, hurt me no more,*
*is what I am longing for!*

*Your hiding away and saying,*
*Go away! The king is not home,*
*and the luring and the harshness*
*of the caretaker is what I am longing for!*

*Every one in existence*
*is given a share of grace.*
*The source of grace and its quarry*
*is what I am longing for!*

*The bread and water of this world*
*is like a treacherous flood!*
*I am a magnificent whale;*
*the sea with no shore is what I am longing for!*

I am shouting
and crying out my grief like Jacob!
The charming face of Joseph of Canaan*
is what I am longing for!

I swear, this town
without you is a prison for me!
Wandering in the deserts and mountains
is what I am longing for!

These weak-spirited companions
make me gloomy.
The company of the Lion of God**
and Rustam*** is what I am longing for!

My soul is tired
of Pharaoh and his tyranny.
The light of the face of Moses of Emran
is what I am longing for!

I am weary of this depressed
and complaining crowd!
Laughter and ecstasy of those drunk with joy
is what I am longing for!

I can express my love
better than the nightingale,
but public envy seals my lips.
Wailing and groaning is what I am longing for!

Roaming about town,
the master was holding a light, saying,
I am weary of the demons and the beasts;
a human is what I am longing for!

The human cannot be found;
we have searched!
What cannot be found

*is what I am longing for!*

*Although poor and needy,
I will not accept small pieces of ruby.
The mine of the finest rubies
is what I am longing for!*

*Hidden from our sight,
everything becomes visible through Love.
The hidden expression of Creation
is what I am longing for!*

*My yearning has gone
beyond dreams and desires.
Transcending time and space,
the essence of love is what I am longing for!*

*My ears heard the story of faith
and were overcome with belief.
Where is the allowance for the eyes?
The image of faith is what I am longing for!*

*One hand holding a cup of wine,
and the other, the curls of the beloved,
a dance like this, in the middle
of the circle, is what I am longing for!*

*The lute is saying,
I am dying from waiting.
The hand, the caress, and the fingers of a maestro,
like Osman, is what I am longing for!*

*I play the song of love,
and my love is a song.
The delicate touch of the fingers
is what I am longing for!*

*O compassionate maestro!*
*Carry on and play the rest.*
*The continuation of the same song*
*is what I am longing for!*

*Rise in the horizon of the east,*
*O Shams! O glory of Tabriz!*
*I have brought the message of Love.*
*The presence of Solomon is what I am longing for!*

---

\* Joseph is one of Rumi's favorite metaphors for divine physical beauty and inner grace. Owing to jealousy from his brothers, Joseph was sold at seventeen as a slave, eventually working under the Egyptian, Potiphar. He was later freed and became the chief adviser to the Egyptian Pharaoh around 1600 BC. His father, Jacob, was deeply grieved by the absence of his favorite son, and he never stopped longing for Joseph until he returned home.

\*\* The title of Ali, the first Imam of Shiites and a powerful follower of Muhammad.

\*\*\* A hero in Persian mythology, whose power was devoted to defending righteousness.

# SPRING OF LOVE

The great twelfth century mystic and Sufi poet, Ruzbehan, calls love the spring of power or an eternal spring. He considers it to be the description of perpetual joy and ecstasy. Another mystic, Iraghi, offers a similar concept in the following poem:

> O winegiver!
> The sun is setting; offer the wine!
> The night is falling
> and the face of the moon is veiled.
> Don't mind the dwindling of the days.
> Offer the wine to behold hundreds of suns
> rising from the sky of the soul.
> If the foundation of life is destroyed, have no fear.
> The spring of love brings joy
> to those who surrender to ecstasy.
> Everyone is drunk
> except for me and my slumbering fortune.
> Let it be awakened
> with the sweet scent of wine.
>
> Iraghi

A day will come when humanity will rule the world with a new recognition of the power of the soul. An awareness will develop beyond the limits of what is currently known to the mind. The human being stands at the brink of a discovery that will lead everyone into a way of relating to each other through a much deeper connection with the heart. This will take place when man allows love to be the guide for reaching a deeper power within.

Divine love blooms as the internal senses become awakened! The profound awareness of the power of the inner senses will be the guiding light that reveals the way, just like the energy that makes plants grow in a new spring. Our bodies will allow us to expand and blossom in a rhythm that reflects the beauty of the soul. Love will finally express itself as an eternal spring and as an infinite well of divinity.

The air of spring softens the body to prepare it for transformation through love. The search for a new beginning invites us to create, and our longing directs us toward love. The power of love is what the earth needs to give birth to its fullness. It touches the deepest center to activate and allow the seeds of life to sprout and grow.

> **Love lifts our hearts within our bodies releasing us to flow in whatever direction love chooses to go. We are called to allow our physical power to be transformed into spiritual greatness and to let our dreams expand beyond what we have ever imagined before. The power of love expresses and affects our relationships as we release the energy and allow it to manifest creatively.**

Rumi sees the longing for love like stormy clouds that are pregnant with divine gifts of providence. The lightning of love strikes in the heart only when it is veiled in the clouds of yearning. The pain of separation is concentrated and condensed into longing, and it cannot be bypassed or eliminated, for it is the stimulus that develops love.

Our transformation through love takes place only when we have developed compassion to allow our love to be for the benefit of everyone and everything. Lightning announces the changes of winter to spring, and the lightning of the heart changes the face of the world from sadness to joy.

The attraction of love is when the beloved appears in the mystery, in much the same way that the clouds become a veil that makes the appearance of the moon more charming. The true joy of life is when the image of the beloved emerges from behind the veil of longing and illuminates the face of the lover, as the earth is bathed in the radiance of the emerging moon.

> *Winter falls upon us*
> *so spring can bring new growth.*
> *Cry the tears!*
> *Allow the longing!*
> *Sadness brings surrender*
> *and a deep desire to be free.*

The spring of love always exists for lovers who are open to receive and allow everything to develop and blossom into beauty. Love's desire, like the seed in the garden, has the capability for growth from within. The hope of development and expansion exists within everyone, and love's desire is the invitation that makes the growth extend to all life. Even if the lover does not reach fullness within an expected time frame, the seeds will still grow to become a garden, and love will eventually offer the inner rewards and its rich fortune.

> **Every hidden seed under the ground has its turn, for one day it will bloom and will push its head out of the ground. It will develop arms that reach and spread sweetness and grace.**

The divine is so infinitely mysterious. It is the beloved who is always bewildering the lover with the deepening of love. We are embraced in the mystery, and the lightning of longing sets loose our unfolding and becoming; we experience the flowering of the soul.

The growth of a seed begins in that life-giving moment, when it surrenders the power of choice to the gentle direction of love. It allows the attraction to draw it out of the darkness and into the light to become what the seed was created to be.

Only love can reveal when to command and when not to command life, for the power of existence is concealed within and is yielded to the true essence of love.

# DĪVĀN OF SHAMS: POEM NO. 536

*The spring of love arrives*
*to transform the dust into a garden.*
*The call is heard from the heavens*
*to bid the wings of soul to fly.*

*The sea becomes filled with pearls.*
*The dry land receives the water of life.*
*The stone becomes a ruby,*
*and the body becomes all soul.*

*If the eyes and the soul of lovers*
*turn into clouds of rain,*
*within the cloud of the body,*
*their hearts flash like lightning.*

*Do you know why the eyes of the lovers*
*become cloudy with love?*
*The beauty of the moon*
*is greatest when it is veiled in the cloud.*

*How lovely it is*
*when those clouds begin to rain!*
*O God, how wonderful it is*
*when the lightning begins to laugh.*

*Out of hundreds of thousands of drops,*
*not a single divine drop falls to earth.*
*If a divine drop were to fall,*
*the whole world would be transformed.*

*The whole earth would change,*
*and those touched by love*
*would become shipmates with Noah*
*and be intimate with the storm.*

*If the storm remains still,*
*the universe would not be set in motion.*
*It is the mysterious flow*
*that moves the world in all directions.*

*O, you living in the world of six directions,*
*accept the gloom and accept the bliss,*
*for those seeds buried in the ground*
*will one day grow into fruitful orchards.*

*Every seed will sprout above the ground*
*and from that source, fresh stems will grow.*
*If a few branches wither and dry,*
*the rest will bear fruit.*

*What is withered will yield to fire,*
*and that flame ignites joy in the soul.*
*What is not this, will become this,*
*and what is not that, becomes that!*

*Something tells me to be silent,*
*you are drunk on the edge of the roof!*
*Whatever bewilders you*
*is bewildered by the Beloved.*

# SPIRIT OF LOVE

The process of surrendering the ego completely to love, which is one of the fundamental concepts of Sufis, is called *Fana*, meaning to die before dying. It is the dissolving of the lover into the beloved. *Fana* is the experience of becoming divine before physical death or the losing of self in order to experience intimacy with the Self. As a whole, *Fana* is the annihilation of the ego.

*Fana* assumes three different forms:
- **Annihilation of the search in what is found.**
- **Annihilation of the recognition in what is recognized.**
- **Annihilation of the observation in what is observed.**

The spirit of love is the longing of the heart to return to its original state of oneness with the beloved to experience a taste of the ecstasy and the tender touch of union. Anyone longing for intimacy experiences the pain of feeling separation of the soul from the source. Even when physical attraction is satisfied with the presence of a certain beloved, the deep longing for divine union still remains inside the heart. Awareness of such a longing by the lover allows the act of *Fana*, and the acquiring of divine attributes.

> *After human characteristics are annihilated,*
> *divine attributes surface and become visible.*
> *Everything turns to devotion;*
> *obscurity turns into clarity.*

Annihilation of the self clears the way for the fire of divine love to spark and ignite in the heart of the lover. Flames of this fire increase through desire, prayer, and meditation. The flames burn in the heart until the lover becomes conscious of one of the divine mysteries, which is the realization that the longing that he feels is actually God's longing for his love.

Sufis believe freedom comes to those who surrender to annihilation of the worldly self. When the mind is free and many of the psychological problems and obsessions have been surpassed, reaching true freedom becomes possible.

> *A true human is like the pupil of the eye*
> *that sees everything but the self.*
> Shah Nemat Ullah Vali

The attraction of the lover to the beloved is like the attraction of a moth to the light, for it intensifies as the light becomes brighter. The fire of love burns inside the heart until nothing is left except the beloved.

> **O Lord, nourish me not with love, but with the desire for love.**
> Ibn e Arabi

Rumi believes the dust was transformed into Adam when it lost its physical characteristics, or what he calls *dustness*. The stone reaches its truest value and turns into a precious jewel when it is freed from darkness. A similar thing happens to a person. The burning away of one's physical attachments creates the movement toward quality and excellence.

Revelations that prophets and saints receive, the inspirations that artists and those who create are given, as well as the level of excellence that champions and athletes are able to reach, all become possible when they are in a state of oneness with divine power. As the longing for union gradually builds within them, their awareness and their talent develops in an accelerating manner and begins to express through them according to their capacity to receive and create.

> *O my friend,*
> *if you are longing to be written on,*
> *become a blank page.*

In the exalted state of oneness, the lover's heart is able to absorb what has been developing through longing and passion. Love gradually shifts into an experience of uniting with the beloved.

# DĪVĀN OF SHAMS: POEM NO. 2429

*The moon and the stars
are revolving about your radiance.
The sun and the wheel of heaven coil
in the loveliness of your labyrinth.*

*O Lord! Am I looking for you,
or is it you looking for me?
O what a shame! As long as I am 'I',
I am one, and you are the other.*

*You diminished both and made us one.
You have created something new,
beyond human or divine.*

*Let there be no feet,
for they lead us to pain.
Let there be no head,
for it leads us to doubt.*

*Some water flows
in the middle of the current,
some freezes on the riverbank.
That moves swiftly;
this moves slowly.
Move freely and remain in the flow!*

*The sun shines on the stone
to break it apart,
revealing the precious ruby
within the stone.*

*The sun of everlasting love
shines into the heart
to make us a slave,
before we become a master!*

The sun tells the unripe grape,
I've come to stop you
from spreading sourness
and brew you to offer sweetness.

The king tells the falcon,
I have covered both your eyes
to keep you from your own nature
so you would see nothing but my face.

I live for you! The falcon says,
I will see nothing but your face
and cherish no one but you!

The rose tells the garden,
I dropped my veil,
so you would sell all your coverings
and become one with us.

Anyone selling gold from here
would be dividing it with others.
Stay faithful and remain with us!
All else is like being a mule.

A man would give
the mule to buy Jesus.
Only a mule would trade
Jesus for a donkey.

Jesus transforms copper to gold.
If gold, he will turn it into a jewel.
If a jewel, he makes it more brilliant
than Venus or the moon.

Don't be a cheap consumer.
Buy the light that shines within!
If you have the virtue of Joseph,
your robe will bear the aroma!

*Dates would grow on a dry branch beyond reason,*
*just like they did for Mary!*
*Greatness develops in the crib without asking,*
*just as it did for Jesus!*

*See the grape without the garden and the vine!*
*See the light outside the day and the night!*
*See the power of the one who speaks the truth.*
*All are ruled by divine justice beyond the law.*

*Don't cry like children*
*from the heat of the water!*
*The bath of the world is heated*
*from the glow of my face.*

*Tomorrow you will see the face*
*become the meal for snakes and rats,*
*and those beautiful eyes*
*will become the palace of ants!*

*The moonlight flows toward the moon,*
*while the wall remains in the shadow.*
*Everything returns to the source.*
*Face only that direction if you can see!*

*Either go toward Tabriz*
*to learn about Shams Uddin,*
*or else, listen to those*
*who describe him well!*

# Attraction of the Beloved

Sufis believe the very purpose of creation is to experience the intimacy with God or to realize God in the deepest possible way. To reach such a state, they have to be continually aware of the attraction that is arising in their hearts that draws them toward the beloved. That divine attraction is called *jazbeh*. It is a feeling that greatly empowers the seeker and produces an ecstatic state.

> **I was a hidden treasure. I desired to be known,
> so I created the universe.**
> The Koran

*Jazbeh* leads to a direct connection with the Beloved. The lover becomes attracted to the essence of what is real. The connection guides him toward divine intimacy, which manifests as a deep love relationship with God. Full human development takes place through *jazbeh* coming from the direction of the beloved and from desire and longing of the lover.

> *No lover could reach intimacy,
> if the beloved were not looking for him.*

One who feels the divine attraction, acquires the attributes and qualities of the divine. As the power of divine finds expression through the heart, the lover is freed from all attachments and assumes an existence in the nature and reality of the beloved. Divine power frees the lover from conflict, hostility, and other negative actions and surrounds and enfolds the whole being in the arms of love. The lover is then able to see the beloved with an inner vision and with deeper insight and is more prepared to receive the virtue and the beauty reflecting the divine nature.

The nature of the human being is to be attracted to beauty and virtue. Both of these develop fully in divine love. The lover falls in love with the beauty and virtue of the beloved, and the beloved falls in love with the lover who is attracted to divine beauty and virtue. There is alchemy in divine love that achieves and creates the mutual balance of those in love.

God states through the Prophet:
**The one who seeks me, finds me.**
**The one who finds me, knows me.**
**The one who knows me, falls in love with me.**
**The one who is my lover; I would be his lover.**
**When I fall in love with him,**
**I would dissolve him into my Self.**

*Jazbeh* or divine attraction is felt in two ways:
- One kind of attraction is through an inward feeling where the lover has the sensation and the pleasure of being attracted. In this case, the lover receives great joy while he is constantly attracted to a source of deeper contentment within. This feeling is sacred to the lover and does not manifest in visible ways. The tendency of the one who has developed an inner attraction is to become reclusive and to feel the desire to be away from the crowd. Shams of Tabriz was from this group.

- The other kind of attraction is one that manifests outwardly. In this case, the lover feels the same type of attraction, but has an urge to manifest it in a form of ecstasy. Because he lives in such extreme joy, that kind of attraction cannot be held inside, for it needs to be expressed in some way. To those who are connected with their rational minds, a person in that state is considered to be mad. Rumi was attracted in a way that left him unable to hold the divine power inside. He needed to allow it to pour through him and express itself, as he did by playing music, dancing, and chanting ecstatic poetry.

Sufis believe the true purification of the soul cannot happen unless the seeker has reached a stable place, a place of assurance. That assurance only comes when the attraction of the beloved becomes the power that guides the person's life. The power and flow of love between the lover and the beloved is the source of divine intimacy. Desire increases as the attraction increases. The union of desire and attraction creates the path of intimacy.

*It is the attraction of water*
*that creates thirst in our soul.*
*Thirst belongs to the water,*
*and the water belongs to the thirst.*
Rumi's Masnavi

The attraction of the beloved is the power that is able to guide the soul without any kind of coercion or without needing any special way to attract it. Without the attraction, the mysterious energy of love would never be manifested into the form of the body. The greatest joy is achieved when attraction to the Divine becomes the path of life.

The attraction of the beloved is a guide, and when it is true, the seeker receives the exquisite wine of the love of God.

# DIVAN OF SHAMS: POEM NO. 3

*O heart!*
*What is your excuse for all these blunders?*
*Such loyalty is offered by the beloved,*
*yet so much treason comes from you.*

*Such kindness is offered by the beloved,*
*yet so much defiance and resistance comes from you.*
*Such grace is offered by the beloved,*
*yet so much fault and failure comes from you.*

*Such attraction is offered by the beloved*
*with sweetness and generosity,*
*yet such jealousy comes from you*
*with so much doubt and suspicion.*

*Why so much variation in taste?*
*To sweeten the bitterness of your soul!*
*Why so many waves of attraction?*
*To elevate you to the pinnacle of purity!*

*When you turn away from doing wrong*
*and begin to look for the truth,*
*the beloved draws you*
*into your freedom!*

*You become frightened of guilt,*
*and you look for escape.*
*Why do you not see that what frightens you*
*also gives you comfort?*

*Even if your eyes are unable to see,*
*you are safe in the arms of love.*
*Sometimes you are rolled like this;*
*sometimes you are tossed like that!*

*Sometimes silver and gold,*
*and sometimes passion becomes your nature.*

Sometimes your soul
receives the light of the divine.

One side is pulled to joy,
the other side to pain.
When caught in a whirlpool,
either you drown or reach for safety.

Pray in solitude.
Weep in the middle of the night,
until you hear a message
from heaven above.

When Shu'eib's* mourning and crying
became unending,
he heard a voice in the dark
from the sky,
If guilty, you are forgiven.
If sinful, your deliverance is given.
If seeking paradise, you have it.
Stop these petitions!

Shu'eib answered,
I am not interested in either this or that!
I am here to see the beloved!
Should the seven seas burn in flames,
I would live to behold that sight!

If I am expelled from seeing that beauty,
and if my weeping eyes are blind,
unable to see the beloved,
then I am in the Inferno!
Heaven is not for me!

Heaven without the beloved is Hell!
I'm burning
in these mortal colors and scents.
Where is the splendor of the Immortal Light?

Stop crying!
Save your eyesight!
Seeing is lost when
crying goes beyond its limits!

If these eyes ever get to see my beloved,
every cell in my body
would turn into an eye.
Why would I worry about going blind?
If these eyes are deprived from seeing the beloved,
let them go blind.

Every person in this world is in search of love!
Some find love in a money bag,
others in the divine light of Shams.

Since we all choose love
within our own capacity,
whether good or bad,
we would regret losing our life for nothing!

Bastami** once asked a follower,
What do you do for a living, clever man?
I'm custodian to a mule for hauling, sir!

Go away, said Bastami,
O Lord, kill his mule.
Let him become custodian to God!

---

* Shu'eib, in accordance to the Koran, was a prophet from Abraham's descent, who appeared shortly before Moses to guide the people of Madyan, a place now located in today's Syria. These people were extremely greedy, deceitful and wicked. They did not listen to Shu'eib's continual plea to be mindful of God, and they seized his belongings and drove him out of their community. The prophet mourned and cried to his God for help, until he became blind. His prayer was answered. One early morning, clouds of smoke and fire appeared in the sky and the whole community was completely devastated by a massive earthquake, and everyone received their punishment for being dishonest.

** Refer to footnote on page 29 on Bastami.

# CARESSED BY THE BELOVED

The beloved in Rumi's poetry is an expansive concept, which does not seem to have any identifiable gender or physical limits. This is mainly due to the fact that the gender of the third person in Farsi is unknown. The reference is to *Ou* (pronounced woo without the 'w'), which can be either *he*, *she*, or *it*. In the poetry of the *Divan of Shams*, the reference to *Ou* as *the beloved* does not identify if Rumi is referring to him, her, or it. One has to ask if it could mean the Divine Beloved, Shams of Tabriz, a female, or is Rumi referring to his mystical love for Shams as a metaphor for his love of God?

**When translating Rumi's poetry into English, deciding on a certain gender for the beloved might not be a true reflection of his intention or a right expression of his deeper concept. For that reason, I have chosen in this book to keep the translations of the verses in the same ambiguous format as the original poetry and refer to Rumi's metaphor for the beloved as merely the beloved.**

Whether male or female, love is beyond gender. The beloved is the spirit of the truth, and the entire universe is bewildered in the light of the truth. The beloved is the concentrated essence of love.

*The beloved is everything;*
*the lover is merely the veil.*
*The beloved is immortal;*
*the lover is mortal.*
*If one seeks anything but the beloved,*
*it is a fleeting passion; it is not love.*
*Love is the flame that consumes*
*all that exists; the beloved alone remains.*

Rumi's beloved is completely independent from all other concepts. Everything is created and developed by the beloved, and life is initiated and flows from it.

The Beloved is the tree of life, and all creation is the fruit.

The beloved is always attracted to the lover's modesty and humility. The pain of longing and the effort of the lover in reaching for union with the beloved is so strong and so delicious that the logical mind could never comprehend its magnetic current.

The power of everything flows from the kingdom of the beloved to the heart of the lover and to all life. It completes a cycle and creates the revolving rhythm of creation. All true joy on earth originates in the beloved and is completed in the lover.

The eyes that behold the beloved could never feel the same when looking at anyone else. The soul that experiences the beloved's intimacy will never be satisfied with bread and water or any sustenance from this world.

> Impoverished is the one who identifies the beloved with trade. Destitute is the one who wants the beloved for status or as a sign of affluence. Foolish is the one who wants to keep the beloved only for the self.
>
> The one who identifies the beloved with trade would live in fear and greed. The one who wants the beloved for affluence or wealth would face affliction and hardship. The one who wants the beloved only for the self would assume the beloved is found, but in truth, it would be only an illusion.
>
> The true lover finds the beloved through the light of love found in the heart. The entire existence of the one captured by that divine love becomes an expression of the beloved. The lover burns with such a fire of love that even the beloved's restraint cannot diminish it.
>
> Ansari

The beloved is the manifestation of the definitive beauty to the lover. The beloved is the treasure of life and the remedy for every broken heart. The beloved is the ultimate quarry of sweetness and the shining jewel of the universe. The divine breath of the beloved breathes out power enough to raise every person, every flower, and every living thing beyond its surroundings.

Every time the lover mentions the name of the beloved, the soul feels the energy and becomes filled with the thrill and the remembrance of love. Even a thought of the beloved can generate an excitement within, quicken the heartbeat, and the light of love can be seen in the eyes of the lover.

> **In the presence of the beloved,**
> **the lover's ego becomes an uninvited guest.**
> **True intimacy will not take place,**
> **until all attachments are released.**
> Attar

True love leads to divine intimacy, which illuminates the lover with divine intellect. Once free from passion for mortal matters, one would no longer feel separate from divine love. When filled with true love, the way is opened for constant connection with God. When divine intellect takes the lead, creativity becomes unlimited.

Intimacy with the beloved becomes a shield that protects the lover from the invasion of any negative force. Being caressed by the beloved bathes the heart in love, and it creates a sanctuary of true comfort.

# DIVAN OF SHAMS: POEM NO. 46

*Weary and consumed by longing,*
*I was caressed by my beloved last night.*
*My wounded soul was set free,*
*when I tasted the sweetness of love.*

*My spirit was lifted at once.*
*I surrendered my life*
*while overflowing with joy,*
*and my vision was filled with light.*

*Love said, don't feel so hopeless,*
*my tired and gloomy one,*
*for my generosity is beyond*
*forgetting those devoted to me.*

*See how boundless divine justice can be.*
*Behold the immeasurable kindness of love.*
*Joseph would never forget those*
*bewildered in love by his presence.*

*Love embraced my spirit,*
*and all my doubts vanished at once.*
*A new and glorious robe of honor*
*was placed on my shoulders.*

*Ignore my stream of tears!*
*Don't judge me as helpless or poor!*
*Behold the elegance*
*of this robe that I am wearing.*

*Those on this eternal quest*
*are unlike anyone else.*
*The soul that is freed from temptation*
*is forever filled with joy.*

*The madness of love is sweeter
when mixed with the beloved's charm,
for the lips bitten by longing
are secretly kissed by the beloved.*

*Love whispers promises to lovers
offering them the splendor of roses.
Love soothes the eyes dried by tears
filling them with the wine of love.*

*Love offers the power of new vision
and the transforming touch of divine generosity.
Even the heart of the wheel of heaven
burns with envy and zeal.*

*Love places the chalice of eternal wine
in the hand of the lover.
Love plays the drumbeat calling the heart
that has flown away like the falcon.*

*Be silent in the holiness of love!
Don't destroy the virtue of silence!
Now that you are caressed by the beloved's sweetness,
stop telling fables and tales.*

*Say nothing!
Speak of nothing!
Don't speak! Don't say a thing!
Keep the door closed to honor love.
Don't reveal that sacred garden in bloom.*

# UNION OF LOVE

The union of love is a melting together of the lover and the beloved into one. The initial movement in that direction is the lover's surrender into the process of losing all sense of self. The next movement happens as the lover acquires the attributes and the characteristics of the beloved. The third and the final movement toward the fullness of the union of love takes place when the lover unites and becomes one with the beloved.

Love is developed completely when the lover and the beloved no longer have individual identities to separate them from each other. At this point of oneness, whatever was blocking or preventing their union has been released and surrendered. When this happens, the ego that is always fighting to prevent the development of love, dissolves and no longer controls the focus of the lover's existence. The lover and the beloved become one in a love that has been purified.

> If you are searching for the precious pearl,
> leave your body and soul on the shore of longing.
> Truth is hidden in the mystery of Love.
> The first movement in that direction is to surrender.
> Unless you wear the crown of disappearance,
> you would not be free to vanish on that path.
> In the union of love, you will be led
> to the door, where you knock to enter.
>
> Sana'i

The union of the lover and the beloved creates a perpetual condition similar to the sovereignty of love itself. Life becomes filled with joy and vitality, and the power of true union begins to manifest creatively.

> *Only the oneness of love and the lover is eternal.*
> *Surrender your heart into this union,*
> *for all else in this world is momentary.*

Everything in the universe is identified through association with something or with someone, either an individual or a group. Among all of them, wholeness is realized most perfectly in the lover, for the lover is the only one who has developed many of the divine attributes. Everything else in this world is transforming and moving toward that exalted level of existence, which is being fully human and fully divine. All human beings are drawn into this transformation as they transcend the focus of physical needs, the desire for ownership, and the attachment to possessions. The mirror holds the reflection of the lover, and when it is purified and untarnished, it reflects the image of the beloved.

> The human soul is more developed than the soul of the animal,
> for it is able to perceive beyond what the animal can grasp.
> The soul of the angel is beyond the human soul,
> for angelic souls are pure and not clouded with feelings.
> Do not be surprised that the soul of the lover
> is exalted beyond the soul of the angel.
> It is love that expands the soul of the lover
> and moves the angels to bow down to man.
> Rumi's Masnavi

Rumi describes to what lengths a lover will go to find union with the source of love. Worldly identity is totally transformed by the power of the deep longing for love, and it dissolves completely in the fullness of union.

The lover continues to become more aware of the true Self and to realize who he truly is in this world, as well as how others perceive him. When completely united with the beloved, the lover loses all worldly sense of the self in love. Everything has been willingly yielded and transformed through the attraction and alchemy of love.

**To be united in love is to be always in the presence of the beloved. Even the awareness of the individual soul dissolves in the greater Soul. Whatever happens to the beloved also happens to the lover. It doesn't matter if the experience is one of joy or one of sadness; the lover experiences it as being one with the beloved.**

In the state of oneness, even pain can be transformed into something felt as sweetness, for love changes the experience in much the same way that a piercing thorn becomes the flowering beauty of the rose.

Lovers have unique qualities that place them above the angels, for they have the divine potential and capability to have an impact throughout the whole universe.

> *As Adam, you have lived*
> *in the arms of the Truth.*
> *Sit on the King's throne*
> *and teach the angels the nature of the Divine.*

As the longing for oneness with the beloved increases and intensifies, it exalts the lover toward a divine union with the beloved. That is when everything changes. It is like standing on a bluff next to the ocean and being overwhelmed by the vastness of the vision. It is like seeing the earth from a new perspective in space and experiencing a feeling of humility at the splendor of something so beyond ordinary existence. It is possible to be lost in the beauty and greatness of it all, much in the same way the lover and the beloved become lost in the vastness of divine love as they experience the ultimate union.

In the following poem, Rumi elevates the human being to a higher level of existence to lift and connect him like a shadow to the Beloved. The lover comes face to face with the entire universe at once to behold and perceive the act of creation itself. That vision embraces and unites us all as a part of the beauty and wholeness. It is the exalted state of being in the presence of pure love.

# DİVAN OF SHAMS: POEM NO. 1397

*Among the thousands of I's and we's,*
*see what a wonderful I, I am!*
*Listen to my cries!*
*Don't cover my mouth!*

*Now that I am out of control,*
*don't obstruct my path,*
*for I'll stomp and smash*
*whatever's in my way!*

*With every breath,*
*I feel my heart is beating with yours.*
*In your joy, I am exuberant!*
*In your sadness, I am in sorrow.*

*If you are bitter, I become bitter.*
*If you are grace, I become grace.*
*My joy is when I am bewildered in your beauty*
*and taste the sweetness of love on your lips.*

*You are the essence of my existence.*
*Who am I? A mirror in your hand!*
*Whatever you do, I will do.*
*I am your irresistible reflection.*

*You are like the cypress in the meadow,*
*and I am your devoted shadow.*
*I am sheltered in your shade*
*under a canopy of roses.*

*If I pick a rose without you,*
*it becomes a thorn in my hand.*
*If I am the thorn,*
*I become the rose in your hand.*

*Every moment without you,
my bleeding heart fills an urn.
Each heartbeat breaks the urn
to drown in your sweet wine.*

*With every breath,
I turn to a new attraction
knowing I will be wounded,
and my robe will be torn open.*

*The tenderness of Salah Uddin\**
*is shining within my heart.
He is my heart's candle in this world.
What am I? Only a candleholder!*

---

\* Salah Uddin was one of Rumi's patrons and a supporting devotee. Rumi is referring here to the tenderness of Salah Uddin as the one whose patronage was brightening the way for him to unite with the Source.

# GARDEN OF THE HEART

Inside every heart, there is a spiritual garden from which great variety of feelings sprout, grow and bloom. We are also the gardener, who maintains and develops the garden. The same as in an actual garden, we pay attention to the quality of the flowers, prevent the growth of weeds, and we bring the garden to its fullest beauty through vigilance and loving care.

*Under the cover of blood,*
*love veils many rose gardens.*
*In total faith,*
*love tenderly guides every lover*
*to the garden of the heart.*

*Reason says,*
*the world is limited in six directions,*
*there is no way out.*

*Love says,*
*there is a way, and I have traveled it many times.*

All the power needed for our life journey is already embedded in the heart. Divine love is the evolutionary driver and the revealing guide. What triggers and moves the heart to begin the journey is the desire for expansion.

Pure love separates the heart from the rational mind. It also removes the attachment and regard for the material world. When we center our love around a particular object or person, we limit the creative power of our heart and its expansion.

**Divine love frees the spirit**
**and unites the heart with the divine essence.**

When we are drawn or attracted to something, whatever is within our hearts flourishes and becomes expressive. There is almost always something unique in that movement meant to expand our awareness.

The most glorious flower that blooms in the garden of the heart manifests as divine love. Divine love is the flowering of the creative energy that empowers everything surrounding it.

Heart has several meanings among the mystics:
- **It is the reflecting Self.**
- **It is the center for our assimilation of the deeper meanings.**
- **It is the treasury of the Divine Secrets.**

Rumi tells us we are the blossoming flowers that one day will become the fullness of the garden of our heart! We are gardeners clearing the way for the light to reflect in this garden, and we are the opening that allows the light to come shining through to flood it with brilliance.

> **I saw my beloved with the eye of my heart, and I asked,**
> **who are you? The beloved said, I am you.**
> Mansur al-Hallaj

Entering the garden of the heart is a very delicate way of becoming. There is an aroma, a fragrance that one experiences when entering. It is a garden of becoming, of appreciating, and of believing. Within the garden, everyone becomes free of the limitations of the material world. Each person becomes delicate like the rose and graceful like the angels without a physical body.

**The joy of flight is experienced when we are no longer feeling the heaviness and gravity of all that keeps us bound to the earth. There is a lightness of being, and a lifting of the spirit that feels like soaring.**

The garden of the heart has no geographical limitations. The expanse of the kingdom of the heart is spread out endlessly with no known boundaries. In the garden of the heart, everything becomes one. The lion becomes like the deer, and the deer becomes like the lion. There is a 'placelessness' where one finds the highest level of freedom.

Only when divine love is realized in the heart, can the creative power of a person truly be expressed. The person becomes the essence of creativity, as well as the source of creation itself. When divine love is allowed in all its glory and splendor to grow and flourish in the garden of the heart, the person becomes the vessel that expresses the true love and the beauty of God.

> *The heart contains the image of the beloved.*
> *Free it from the toxic effects of worldly passions,*
> *for the divine image is extremely delicate.*

In the garden of the heart, we are not meant to look on the ground to find the answers in work, material world, or in whatever we own. We are not created to live at that lower level of existence. We are invited and encouraged to see ourselves in a much higher dimension.

Awareness of what is going on inside the heart and knowing the way it works for our growth is the most important and most revealing pathway to follow to bring true joy to life.

**Rumi suggests that all the answers that we need to fully enjoy our life can be found growing and developing within the garden of our own hearts.**

When we become aware of the depth and beauty of our own hearts and continue to explore them further, we discover the deeper hidden feelings, which enable us to mature while we keep a close relationship with our heart. This is the way to transform conflicts and difficulties into bliss. Love is the guide that leads us to the truth, and it is constantly making itself known to us through the heart.

## DIVAN OF SHAMS: POEM NO. 2444

When you enter the garden of the heart,
you become fragrant like the rose.
When you fly toward heaven,
you become graceful like the angel.

If you are burned like oil,
you become brilliant.
When you become thin like hair in yearning,
joy leads the way.

You'll be the kingdom and the king.
You'll be paradise and the guardian angel.
You'll be infidelity, and you'll be faith.
You'll be the lion, and you'll be the deer.

You leave a place for placelessness.
ou leave the self for selflessness.
You lose your vessel and your feet.
You flow like water in the stream.
You'll be pure like the heart and the soul.
You'll be the vision of the invisible.
You'll be bitter and sweet.
You'll take on the nature of the wine.

You'll stroll on water and land
like the Christ.
You'll uncurl the whirlpool
and free your course.

You'll sweeten every sour.
You'll become the close to every far.
You'll be no shade to the light,
when, like the universe,
you expand to the infinite.

*Be the king who has made his own kingdom.*
*Be the moon that has made her own summit.*
*How much longer*
*will you coo like a pigeon?*

*Empty your head of all mortal lusts,*
*and become life without breath.*
*You will not call out for God anymore,*
*for you have become immersed in God.*

*You'll be the Source of the light for every home.*
*You'll be the rose in every garden.*
*You'll be I without the self,*
*when you become you without you!*

*Stop looking down so much!*
*Lift your head up and shout with joy,*
*until you become blissful, fresh, and laughing*
*like a branch of persimmon.*

*You will not be looking for light;*
*you'll be shining by yourself.*
*You'll be nourishing your subjects like the king.*
*You'll brighten the darkness like the moon.*

*When you are not desperate for life, you give life.*
*When you are not in pain, you become the cure!*
*You will no longer look for solutions,*
*for you become the solution!*

# HEART OF THE TRUTH

Heart is the image of the soul. It is the source of inner knowing and the proper guide in one's life. Heart is the wellspring of imagination and the source of true faith. Creativity develops and flows through the heart as the expression of love.

**Heart is the container, the sacred chalice that holds the divine secrets.**

Divine truth is the mystery permeating the physical world. Connection with it is through the heart. Heart turns duality into oneness. It is the essence of life and love as the two become unified. It harbors a divine light that reveals and illuminates the truth.

> **Heart is the center of union.**
> **It is the home of serenity and oneness.**
> **Although blind to it, the heart**
> **is the ultimate tabernacle of the truth.**
> **Even though buried inside the clay,**
> **the heart is the expression of light and darkness.**
> **Once the covering of clay is removed,**
> **the heart is bathed in the light of truth,**
> **even in its lowliness.**
>
> Attar

No matter how connected we are with ourselves or how detached from our inner reality, divine love always exists inside our hearts.

Sufis believe the heart is the sanctuary of God's love. When it is purified of all the natural contaminations of the corporal world, divine love appears within it and becomes the reflection of the image of the beloved.

> **I used to have a heart that attended**
> **to all my troubles gracefully.**
> **It was a gentle and prudent companion**
> **and a support for everyone**
> **connected with their hearts.**

> **Whenever I fell into the vortex of grief,**
> **it tenderly guided me to the shore of freedom.**
> **I lost my heart in the kingdom of the beloved.**
> **O Lord, what a majesty that was!**
>
> Hafiz

The soul is always interested in taking the ego into its own realm, while the ego wants to do the reverse and break away from the soul. This struggle is constant. Sometimes, the soul wins and elevates the ego to purity; other times, the ego wins and draws the soul into impurity. The heart is always following the stronger of the two, until one completely takes over the other, in which case, the heart follows the victor. If the winner is the soul, eternal joy exalts the heart and transforms the person into a true believer. If the opposite happens, the heart becomes doubtful and a source of confusion and separation.

The struggle between the ego and the soul is at the center of many religious teachings. The question arises, how can the heart always be right, if it is controlled by the ego? Organized religions teach that when we lose our soul, we fall into hell instead of going to heaven. When we feel confusion and separation, the heart guides us to let love lead us home. The heart is a guide in all choices, good or bad, light or dark, conscious or unconscious, in pain or in ecstasy, bringing all opposites to union through love. No wonder Rumi says the heart is right even when it seems wrong.

> *Every moment, a new sign*
> *arrives to attract the soul.*
> *A new image appears*
> *inside the heart*
> *inviting it*
> *to return to its original home.*

In the eternal realm, where duality does not exist, our true nature is divine consciousness. The lover and the beloved are the same in that realm, and the mirror is not separate from what is in front of it. The mirror, in reality, is reflecting its own consciousness.

> Not being able
> to fall in love with his own beauty,
> God created a mirror to reveal
> his own hidden grace.
> That mirror is the heart.
> Look into your heart
> to behold the grace of the Beloved.
>
> Attar

The act of polishing the heart like a mirror is by developing the desire to expand, which is the essence of creativity. Life by itself is a process of constantly creating. Responding to the desire to polish our own mirror is to learn the art of living. A life that is predetermined and pre-planned becomes uncreative and without excitement. To be truly creative is to be spontaneous and open to allow life to express itself freely through the heart.

> *The shore of the heart is infinite.*
> *The universe is concealed in it.*
> *O ocean of the heart, tell me,*
> *who harbors the vast desert of my chest?*

Heart is the wayfarer of the world. It is the moth of the soul circling about the light of the beloved. Rumi describes the heart as having the same qualities as the beloved and calls it the lion of the jungle of truth, the army of truth, and the palace and haven of divine grace.

Heart is the source and center for every image, yet it takes no form of its own. It is the caretaker of the spirit. It is filled with infinite qualities. Only love can recognize its true value.

# DĪVĀN OF SHAMS: POEM NO. 1377

*Greetings from my heart
to you who are always with me,
hidden inside as the heart.
You are the compass of my life.
My course is your way,
no matter where I go.*

*You exist everywhere and in everything
always watching over us.
My soul brightens in the darkness
when I speak your name.*

*Sometimes like a cherished falcon,
I fly in the vastness of your palm.
Other times like a homing pigeon,
I return to the splendor of your kingdom.*

*If you are not with me,
how come my heart is always breaking?
If you are with me,
why am I forever longing for you?*

*Far beyond the body,
there is an opening from my heart into yours.
Through that opening,
I send you secret messages like the moonlight.*

*O glorious sun,
I feel the caress of your light from far away!
You are the soul in every longing soul.
Let me lose myself in you.*

*I polish the mirror of my heart
to be your reflection.
I make my ear the receiver
for the tenderness of your words.*

*You are in the ear.*
*You are in the mind.*
*You are in every burning heart.*
*What am I saying? You are I.*
*This is my way to describe you!*

*O heart, remember*
*the beloved's constant reminder,*
*whatever is diminished in you is completed by me.*

*O solution in every solution,*
*pay attention and observe!*
*See among all your images*
*the one I am presently reflecting.*

*Sometimes straight like the letter, I,*
*sometimes shaped like other letters.*
*One moment I see you formed;*
*the next moment I see you formless.*

*Even if you are far away,*
*you are still a pawn in my hand.*
*I am in constant control*
*of the hidden expressions in you!*

*O my king, Hessam,\**
 *let the beloved know,*
*I burnish my soul into the sheath*
*for the sword of your compassion.*

---

\* Hessam Uddin Chalapi was Rumi's devoted apprentice and the one who later wrote down the verses of the Masnavi as Rumi dictated to him.

# HOUSE OF LOVE

The house of love is the manifestation of the soul.

In this house, the light of truth shines and love is generously shared.

The door to the house of love is to remain always open. True spiritual leaders have given their lives to make this fact known. The house of love is where true faith develops.

The house of love is delicate and bright inside, and it is filled with joy. It is so expansive that the whole world is bewildered in it.

What kind of house are we creating with the thoughts and desires of our own life? The great mystics continually reveal wonderful images to help us visualize and feel what the experience might be like.

> **Do not be fascinated by gaining too much knowledge in order to consider yourself a fully informed person. Do not be trapped into spending too much of your time in prayer and worship so that you would be considered devout or a hermit. These all entail much pain and torture, and they can be excessive and prideful attempts for recognition. Be content with the necessary knowledge needed for your life and do the basic prayer and worship required by your belief system. Let your primary focus be to spend your life purifying your spirit and opening the door to your heart to make it a true house of love where everyone is welcome.**
> Nasafi

The house of love is a place of God's treasures and is located beyond the celestial dimension and beyond the firmament. Even the Garden of Eden is modest in front of the majesty of the house of love. The beauty of the world is initiated and flows from the house of love. True solitude can only be realized and experienced in the house of love.

Enlightenment develops naturally in the house of love. A divine light of recognition is placed inside every person so they are able to distinguish between love's reality and much of the nonsense the world offers. This knowledge cannot be obtained from books. It is discerned through the vision and perception of love.

> **The body's task is to expand its beauty and richness;**
> **the heart's task is to develop friendship and love.**

The master of the house of love is capable of offering a hand to help those who are trapped in the physical world and guide them toward the spiritual realm and the eternal world. The master of the house of love has been given a spiritual power and a celestial kingship. He is not associated with the external appearance or the visible identity that others can see. His whole existence is dedicated to bringing spiritual joy to others.

The heart is always seeking sweetness. It runs away from sorrow and grief.

When a heart is filled with love, it becomes warm and full of energy. It loses all fear or shyness and has the courage to be open and free.

Ruzbihan has classified those who are connected with their hearts into four groups:
- The devout whose heart is tired from fervent prayer.
- The frightened whose heart is broken from too many tears.
- The disciple whose heart is given to service.
- The lover whose heart has dissolved in the beloved.

When the heart is filled with love, we feel the ecstasy, and it affects everyone around us. We become divine chalices filled to the brim and running over. We stand at a threshold every day of our lives. Will we meet the day with reserve and fear or with the courage of an open heart? Love spreads and expands touching everyone with joy.

> *The one with a heart*
> *is like a blossoming tree*
> *in the middle of the garden of faith.*
> *What is the use of a dried up tree?*
> *It burns and becomes fire.*

The love we experience is not determined by what someone else does or does not do. It does not rest in the hands of others, and it does not depend on whether someone else loves us or not, as we have been led to believe by those who offer illusions for sale. It lies within our own power to choose to become love, to be love, and to build a house of love where every one is welcome to share the wonder of laughter and song that flows from an open heart.

With all the descriptions of the house of love, Rumi believes that the true description of the heart is beyond what words can express. The magnificence of the heart can leave us speechless.

> *Silence! Words can not describe the qualities of the heart,*
> *even if you had two tongues on every tress of your hair.*

# DIVAN OF SHAMS: POEM NO. 332

*What kind of a house is this?*
*Why is it always filled*
*with music and songs?*
*Let's ask the master of the house.*

*Why is there a carved idol*
*if this is the house of God?*
*Why is there such divine light*
*if this is a pagans' tavern?*

*Inside lies a treasure*
*beyond the limits of time and space.*
*This house and its master*
*are only a veil for a divine cause.*

*Lay no hand on this house,*
*for it is a talisman.*
*Don't say a word to the master,*
*for he is reeling in ecstasy at night!*

*The dust and rubbish of this house*
*is all musk and perfume.*
*Every sound heard from it*
*is all music and songs of joy.*

*The truth is anyone finding*
*the way into this house*
*is the sultan of the earth*
*and the Solomon of time.*

*O master, look down*
*from the roof of this house,*
*for embedded in you*
*is a glory that glows from your face.*

*I swear to your soul, that apart
from seeing your face,
everything else in this world
is only fable and fantasy.*

*The garden is bewildered
in every leaf and every blossom.
The birds are bewildered in
every seed and every snare.
This is the master of the universe
manifesting as Venus and Mars.
This is the house of Love
reaching beyond time and space.*

*The soul has taken your image
into its heart like a mirror.
The heart is caressing
the curl of your hair like a comb.*

*My love! Meet me
in the heart of my soul
where the maidens
lose consciousness at Joseph's arrival.*

*Everyone in this house is drunk.
No one is aware
who is who or what is what
among those who arrive.*

*It is a bad omen to sit by the door!
Come in at once!
Those who stay on the threshold
cast a shadow inside the house.*

*Worldly drunks gather
in groups of two or three.
Thousands become one in divine drunkenness.*

*Enter the lion's jungle!*
*Don't think about getting hurt!*
*Fearful thoughts are*
*phantoms of the mind!*

*No one is harmed in this jungle.*
*Everything is compassion and love.*
*It is your fear holding you back*
*like a bar behind the door.*

*O heart! Be silent!*
*Don't set fire to this jungle!*
*Draw back your tongue,*
*for your words ignite fire!*

# DIVINE PEARL

According to traditional Islamic cosmology, the universe is made of nine spheres enfolded and centered on the earth. The hierarchy of these spheres is set in accordance with different levels of the spiritual journey of man.

> *You enfolded nine emerald spheres in space*
> *to bring the face of earth into orbit.*
> *O water, what are you washing?*
> *O wind, what are you seeking?*
> *O thunder, why are you roaring?*
> *O sphere, why are you turning?*

The outer sphere is *Arsh* or the divine crown, beyond which is the invisible world or eternity. The four physical elements: earth, water, fire, and air originate from the invisible realm and are mixed throughout the revolution of the nine spheres. The three realms are minerals, plants, and animals and are produced from the four elements. The soul, while it is eternally in the invisible realm, expands as the spirit through the descending levels of the universe to become entrapped in its darkest residence, the physical body.

According to Rumi, the spirit first appears on earth as the mineral, and then it starts its ascent to return to its original place in eternity. This journey is taken in successive stages of transformation from mineral to plant, plant to animal, and animal to man. As soon as it takes on the complete form of a human being, the spirit is ready to break away from the darkness of the body and take the final journey of returning home.

> *I died as mineral and became a plant.*
> *I died as plant and rose to animal.*
> *I died as animal, and I was human.*
> *What should I fear?*
> *When was I ever less by dying?*

The journey of the spirit takes thousands of years of going with joy through the experiences of longing as the guiding light. Making the journey on the spiritual path is the process through which the spirit is gradually able to free itself from the confinement of the ego.

The journey of the spirit begins in the physical realm by our being present to others through offering great compassion and tenderness for everyone and everything.

**We awaken to the truth that we are here to discover the joy and the fullness of life!**

The recognition that we have come from the kingdom of the Beloved fills our eyes with the light of love and casts a beam of light over a great distance. We carry an aura of the light of love.

After the spirit has transcended the various stages of physical and spiritual transformation, it is reunited with the divine Soul. A new awareness prepares and makes the soul ready for the next journey.

Divine essence is placed in everything. If we only look at the outer covering, we miss the pearl or the jewel inside, not only in others, but also in ourselves. We need to look with eyes that see the unseen to feel the invisible. We are travelers, sometimes called wayfarers, and we come here only temporarily to be able to share and spread joy.

Rumi's use of the phrase, *the four mothers* in the following poem, refers to the four elements of earth, water, fire and air. The *seven fathers* refers to the seven spheres encircling Earth, inside *Arsh*, the ninth sphere.

Love is the ultimate power that gives us freedom and creates the longing for the light to brighten the way for us to find our direction. As we follow love in our movement toward the fullness of life, we gradually become the very essence of existence! We are the divine pearl, which is held in divine hands reaching out to offer us the deeper meaning of our lives.

# DIVAN OF SHAMS: POEM NO. 1390

*I have returned.*
*I have returned.*
*I have come once more*
*from the Kingdom of the Beloved.*

*Look into me!*
*Look into me!*
*I have come here*
*with great compassion for you!*

*I have come with joy!*
*I have come with joy!*
*I have come in utter freedom.*
*It took thousands of years*
*before I began to speak.*

*I will go back.*
*I will go back.*
*I was up.*
*I will go up.*

*Release me!*
*Release me!*
*I am here seeking only a shelter.*

*I was the divine bird.*
*See how I became earthbound!*
*I did not see the trap!*
*Suddenly, I was caught in it!*

*I am the pure Light, my son.*
*I am not a handful of worthless dust.*
*I am not just an empty shell.*
*I am a regal pearl formed in this world!*

*Close your eyes to see and become aware of me.*
*Perceive me with eyes that see the unseen.*
*Come into the mystery to find me.*
*I am a carefree visitor here for you.*

*I am beyond the four mothers.*
*I am beyond the seven fathers.*
*I am a jewel mined from the divine quarry*
*transported here for a visit.*

*My beloved is revealed in the market,*
*so clever and aware.*
*Why else would I be buying?*
*I am here seeking my Beloved.*

*O Shams of Tabriz!*
*When will you gaze into the whole Universe?*
*I have come with a weary soul and heart,*
*to the valley of annihilation.*

# FLOW OF LIFE

Existence in its fullness is already complete. Everything that is created is endowed with all that it needs for the continuation of its own life. By surrendering to the flow of whatever is coming to us, regardless if it is causing pain or joy, we accept the unfolding as a part of the chain of cause and effect. Resistance to change can cause us not to try something new. When we resist, we become inflexible in our beliefs and lose our ability to respond. Mystics tell us that the secret to good fortune flows from surrender and selflessness.

> **In this world made of land and sea,**
> **nowhere is as vast as surrender.**
> Attar

The one who surrenders to the flow of life is not shaken by every change or every new thing that comes along. The focus of such a person is often on the beauty of life and the energy of love. There is a true selflessness that becomes the guide for this life. When a major change happens, the person is flexible enough to make the adjustment.

> **The entire existence is the expression and manifestation of God, which holds the infinite images of divine attributes and characteristics. The grace of God is like the flow of water, and the universe is like the river. Although a drop of water that is flowing in any part of the river is different from the previous drop, the grace of God remains constant. Everything in existence is continually benefiting from God's infinite grace. Only the conditions change from one level to another, and new circumstances evolve every moment for new possibilities.**
> Gheisari

Everything in the universe is encoded with hidden messages, calling us to be in the flowing stream of energy that is constantly renewing the fullness of life. Spring warms the ground, melts the ice, causes the water to flow and seeds to sprout. Everything reaches toward the light to let the power of life expand and welcome its blooming.

> *Hundreds of thousands like us*
> *are bewildered in the beauty of the beloved*
> *where all bewildered*
> *spirits and hearts are dissolved.*

Just like a garden, we experience the variety of the ways we live in the spring of our own renewal. Our right to life is a gift granted by the divine court, and our creator endows the right to everyone equally. It is the same way that the right is given to every plant in the garden regardless of how they look or what form they take. We are given the right of the sunlight, the rain, the rich soil that nurtures us, and the joy of unfolding to become like the sensuous and delicate blossoms of spring.

> *Tell me the truth, I asked love,*
> *what are you?*
> *I am the everlasting life, love said,*
> *I am the recurring joy of living.*

In the same way as the garden becomes a reflection of the gardener, we are the living creation of the heart of a loving creator. We are the true expression of the spring of life giving birth to itself! Everything is new, and the revelation rivals the brightness of the galaxies. Sometimes, we are hidden behind the veil, like a plant hibernating in the darkness of winter. The voice of life calls us out into the light to discover the joy of living as it does for plants in the spring.

**Once we become aware of our own truth, nothing can ever imprison us again. No tomb can silence the spirit.**

The real flow of life is found in the awakening of the heart, and freedom is found in the awareness of the deeper spring within us. Our life is given to us as a divine gift of God. Our very existence is the proof of the generosity and goodness of a creator that calls us to life out of the darkness and into the light.

The key to transformation from the darkness into the light is hidden inside us. We need to be content with this transformation within ourselves, to allow it to change us. We will then be able to share its fruits with others, not just by the words coming from our mouths.

**Every person has to find the voice of love within themselves.**

Rumi discerned:
Every precious image has been hidden behind the veil of the heart. The garden becomes the mirror reflecting the riches inside. What is seen is the reflection of the heart and not the mirror. The mirror can only reflect images. It can never reveal the soul.

Divine wisdom is concealed inside everything in the universe. Rumi asserts that deep wisdom will always endeavor to reach out to make itself known. When we allow love to radiate from us, we are witness to the glory of the expression of divine wisdom. It does not reflect in the words, but in the transformed life that shines through us. We move out of the way, and we let the divine voice have its way with us. We let love speak through our heart.

Only God expresses creative power, and we witness it by letting it be revealed through us, doing everything we can to learn enough to cooperate with it. It is through our surrendering to the flow that we allow it to happen. We let ourselves be transformed by love, not to serve a particular beloved but to serve everyone.

# DIVAN OF SHAMS: POEM NO. 782

*Are you aware that*
*sweetness is found*
*everywhere in town?*

*Are you aware that*
*winter is gone*
*and spring has come around?*

*Are you aware that*
*sweet basil and the carnation*
*are whispering in the garden*
*and laughing about*
*how simply everything is found?*

*Are you aware*
*the nightingale*
*has come back from its flight*
*singing out messages of love*
*to spread delight with every sound?*

*Are you aware*
*when the tree*
*heard the news from the rose*
*that the garden is revived;*
*it stretched out its arms*
*and began to dance in bloom?*

*Are you aware that*
*the soul is drunk*
*from the spring wine*
*and has been dancing in the harem*
*of the Sultan in sheer joy?*

*Are you aware that*
*the tulip is blushing*
*from its excited heart?*

*Are you aware that
the rose is the sacred
forte of every gathering?*

*Are you aware that
when the cold and crazy
thief of winter saw the arrival
of the guardian of spring,
it ran away to hide?*

*Everything in the garden
is granted the right
from the Divine Court
to appear for our delight.*

*Everything is here
to make the earth green and alive
as a haven for our life.*

*The cascading charm
and the elegance
created in the garden every year,
becomes a hundred times
more thrilling
than the year before.*

*Endless newcomers
arrive spiraling
from the unknown,
making every star
in the galaxy wander
in the wake of their beauty.*

*The dethroned narcissus
reigns over
the meadow again.
Every arriving bud
is insightful and aware*

*like Jesus in the cradle.*

*The feast of those in bliss
becomes charming again,
and once more the wind
spreads the spring wine
across the arid garden.*

*Every precious image
has been hidden
behind the veil of the heart.
The garden
becomes the mirror
reflecting the riches inside.*

*What is seen
is the reflection of the heart;
it is not the mirror.
Mirrors can only
reflect images.
They can never reveal the soul.*

*All those who were dead
respond to a divine call to life.
All their doubts
are transformed to faith
in the flow
of the gift of blessing.*

*What remains
buried in the soil
will always endeavor to reach out.
No one truly alive
can ever be pawned
to a prison or a tomb.*

*Be silent!
Hear these words from within,*

*I can explain this
better than you!
Draw back your tongue.
The Eternal Word is already spoken!*

*Only the King's lips
can speak the eloquence
that expresses life.
Your inadequate words
might cause denial!*

# FINDING THE PATH

Early Sufis, who lived soon after the Prophet, Muhammad, spent most of their lives the same way as the rest of the Moslems, observing and following the Islamic code of conduct called *Shariat*. These rules were quite strict dealing with the need to conform to the established rules, rituals, and ceremonies dictated by religious laws. They were mainly concerned with the punishments for the infidels and rewards for the believers.

From the ninth century on, Sufis began to recognize that spiritual growth couldn't be achieved by following only *Shariat*. Although *Shariat* was essential for guiding their conduct, it was not enough to develop their spiritual growth. As a result, they adopted other spiritual practices beyond *Shariat*, known as *Tarighat*, meaning the path. It is the inner path that helps develop a spiritual connection for the Sufis, as well as for all other esoteric mystical paths, especially for the path of love.

> *Shariat is the belief.*
> *Truth is the pearl.*
> *Tarighat is the path connecting the two.*
> Shabestari

*Shariat* is the condition or creed in which the seeker has to live in accordance with the doctrine of religion as it is strictly laid down in the laws. *Tarighat* is the condition of renunciation, which eventually leads to the next stage, in which the seeker is granted revelation of the nature of the Truth or of the Beloved.

*Tarighat* is the experience and process of dealing with human relationship. This has to do with developing an understanding and awareness of what a person needs for personal growth in his unique situation and life. It is not about following certain practices or doing or not doing certain things in order to be spiritual. It is using the freedom to find the creative path suited to a person's own nature. It is like an artist developing a personal expression or creative style in his art. We search for a personal and creative path of spiritual growth.

The spiritual development of a person is discovered and activated through recognition of the way of others. Time is often spent learning the different approaches that are available. Mystics and Sufi masters point the way toward certain paths that they have experienced. They scatter the seeds of growth inviting others to develop them in new ways. Every person must choose the path that is best suited for his or her own nature. An appropriate companion or a guide is absolutely necessary to offer guidance and validation along any path of nurturing the spirit.

> **A guide is needed; don't journey alone!**
> **Don't enter the ocean blinded by pride.**
> **Guidance is necessary to find your path.**
> **A guide is a shelter in your search.**
> **Since you can't discern a cliff from the road,**
> **how can you cross without a cane?**
> **The road is long, and you are blind.**
> **Your guide keeps watch over the way.**
> Attar

Regardless of whom one chooses to follow, the guidance is always limited to the awareness or the knowledge of the guide. When seekers turn to someone whose awareness truly comes from the heart, they have tapped into an infinite source of guiding light.

As one begins the journey of self-realization, it is often initiated by searching outside of the self. When disappointed by some discovery, a person would finally turn within and listen to the heart for answers. Keeping a close connection with those who have already experienced the journey into the heart helps the person to find the inner path. When he looks for answers in a direction apart from the heart, confusion develops, doubt appears, and trust fades away.

Finding the path into the heart does not necessarily need a sage or a master as a guide. Sufficient guidance is usually received through those who are connected with divine wisdom through their hearts. Once the spiritual guide is accepted, the follower needs to develop the same charity and gentleness within the heart as the guide.

> **When you hear words
> of those connected with the heart,
> don't label it wrong.
> You are not able
> to recognize the truth, my dear;
> that is what is wrong.**
> Hafiz

The person who is connected with the heart is totally free and truly wants to offer and share that freedom with everyone. Such a person has no interest in imposing personal ideas or personal will on the followers. In fact, the person connected with the heart has no will, because the will has been surrendered, and the personal human will has become the divine Will.

Rumi teaches us that connecting with the heart has little to do with direction or advice that tells anyone what to do. This type of guidance is about leading the human spirit to the divine soul. It is about reaching for the deepest level of development that humanity can reach.

Mystics see the spiritual life as a course in developing an inner awareness, not a series of strict instructions. As Rumi would say, it is not about this or that or about being right or wrong. The spiritual way or *Tarighat* is about embracing one's own destiny and being alert to recognize the divine clues for personal guidance.

> **Sell your cleverness and buy bewilderment!**
> Rumi's Masnavi

According to Rumi, finding our true direction is to be utterly bewildered in order to discover clues which we wouldn't otherwise perceive. By listening to our dreams, to our insights and intuitions, and to the words that attract us, clues to our path appear to clarify the way and reveal the direction. The purpose of the spiritual path is to find a freedom in life that is not available in the physical world.

What Rumi calls *the grace of the spiritual guide* is a grace given to the heart, which is our greatest source of consciousness. Being in the presence of those who are connected with the heart develops inner power for the wayfarers to be in touch with the higher Self or their own hearts.

> Those attentive to the heart become aware of the mysteries. The purification of the heart is needed to receive and see the divine reflection.
>
> Lahiji

Only those connected with their hearts find their place in the kingdom of the Beloved. Separation from the heart leads to confusion, the loss of balance in life and a lack of awareness.

> *Close the door of hell!*
> *Imprison your greediness!*
> *Open the door to heaven!*
> *Lighten up your heart!*

The following poem is a disclosure of truth in the clarity of Rumi's creative language. By connecting with the heart, we find balance and meaning as we discover oneness with the self and with others. When we learn to follow the heart, we find a path of great joy!

# DIVAN OF SHAMS: POEM NO. 563

*O Heart!*
*Stay close to those who know about the heart.*
*Choose the shade of a tree*
*that is in constant bloom.*

*Don't meander aimlessly*
*among the herb sellers and potion venders.*
*Go directly to the shop*
*that sells nothing but sugar.\**

*Find your true balance,*
*or you will be deceived.*
*One would offer a fake coin,*
*and you will mistake it for gold!*

*He would deceive you*
*to sit by the door and wait for his return.*
*Don't sit waiting for promises,*
*for that house has another door.*

*Don't sit waiting by every boiling pot*
*to have your plate filled!*
*Not every boiling pot*
*is cooking what you want.*

*Not every sugar cane is filled with sugar.*
*Not every down has an up.*
*Not every eye has vision.*
*Not every sea contains pearls.*

*Oh singing nightingale!*
*Sing your heart out!*
*The moaning of desire*
*pierces the heart of the stone.*

*Lose your head!*
*Not a single thread that has a head*
*can go through the eye of the needle.*

*The awakened heart is like a lantern.*
*Keep it sheltered*
*from the turbulence*
*of the winds of desire.*

*When you go beyond the turbulence,*
*you will reach the Divine Spring,*
*where you will forever be intimate*
*with one who nourishes your soul.*

*With your soul nourished,*
*you will be like a tree in spring*
*that always bears new fruit,*
*for its movement flows*
*from within the heart.*

\* Aflaki, one of the writers of Rumi's earliest accounts, completed in 1353, describes the following story related to this verse:

> Shams Uddin Malati, one of Rumi's disciples said that one day, during his discourses, Our Master suddenly said, "I love everything about Shams Uddin Malati immensely, but he has one fault, that I hope God will remove from him." Malati goes on to say, "I begged Our Master to tell me about that fault and he told me my fault is that I believe God is in everything on earth, which is why I run after any phantom searching for the truth:
>
> > Since many evils have a human face,
> > one should not shake just any hand.
> > Since you don't have the eyes to see what is hidden,
> > you assume there is a treasure inside everything."
> > Rumi's Masnavi
>
> Malati continues to say, "I recognized the fault and repented with total clarity, for I used to attend every sermon, go to every lecture, and listen to whoever had something to say. I was always searching with full sincerity for help in finding the way. Ever since our Master revealed what was to open my eyes, I have stayed away from all those gatherings. I realized that the truth about the Truth is not lost, and I found the Path. That day, our Master repeated this verse so everyone would remember:
>
> > *Don't meander aimlessly… Don't meander aimlessly…*"

# BEYOND THE BODY

A human being, to Rumi, is a multi-dimensional being that not only lives in the body; it exists simultaneously in various realms beyond the body.

To be human is to be of divine origin, for the spiritual nature has a far greater value and importance than the material existence. The body's function is to utilize what exists in the material world to reach its full potential. It is wrong to regard the physical self as superior to the spiritual self. Human obligation is to surrender to the true Self to connect and benefit from the power that exists beyond the body.

When we consider ourselves only as physical beings, we limit our full human potential. The soul is meant to benefit from every circumstance. While living on this earth, we are to enjoy physical experiences, at the same time as we are protecting our soul from becoming a slave to the material world. Our life purpose is to extend the reach of our mind, imagination, capacity, and our relationship with our true Self beyond all limits. This expansion is necessary if we are to reach our fullest potential in the present embodiment.

**The human world is composed of two distinct realms:**
   **- The one related to the daily reality or the ego.**
   **- The absolute reality or the true Self.**

Our reality is the world we see and experience daily. It is the reality that is governed by circumstance. The absolute reality or the truth is beyond our certainty, which we refer to as God, the Beloved, or the true Self.

Our physical reality is made of an infinite substance or energy called spirit, which is contained within our living body. This is different from our human soul, which is eternal and pre-existing. Spirit grows and expands and is developed as an integral aspect of our life on earth. In mystical terms, spirit is connected with the individual while the soul is divine and infinite.

> Know that the mystics call the reality of being human, spirit. Spirit is aware of everything from a single detail to the whole and is knowledgeable of the self as well as the true Self. Some call spirit *Nafs* or ego.
>
> Nasafi

Connection with the spirit is through the heart. Spirits are able to communicate and blend with each other. The spirit that is able to connect with love has the body as its servant rather than as a burden to carry. All the organs of the body are following the command of the spirit. This has great significance in healing and in how we manifest our physical body. Love becomes an agent of healing, a guide in creation, and the energy that connects us with the Divine.

> *The same way that the dust lies under the wheel to support its roll, the body's organs are submissive to the spirit.*

The spirit is what separates the living body from the corpse. It is the source of intelligence, consciousness, and the ability to feel or perceive. This is a powerful indication that we are eternal beings. We are more than immanent in human evolution, for we are also in development with the universe. The joy and sorrow of this world flow from the values we have either heard and trust, or we have formed speculative and vain opinions of our own. Rumi tells us to break through these limits and go beyond what we perceive as safe boundaries, both tangible and conceptual.

> *Now that it does not fit within any limit,*
> *I break every limit.*

If problems that relate to the physical world are not ours, then why do we experience so many dichotomies in our life? What causes us to perceive the rain as a limitation, if we do not have a roof above our head?

**We need to experience separation in order to enjoy intimacy. We break away from our self to experience being us.**

Before taking on a material existence, man dwelt in the realm of formlessness as the Soul and was united with other spiritual beings. While man developed, his soul became enclosed in a physical shell, so he could exist as body and spirit in a material world while his true being remained in the spiritual world as a divine companion.

As humans, we pass through an evolution within the material world and continue our progress. The spiritual being remains in pure spirit form, while man passes through the process of evolution in the material world. Sometimes, the spirit of a person remains on earth after death and maintains consciousness and mind without the body. This spirit is what some would consider a ghost or a disembodied spirit.

**The Divinity, which is the sum of all perfection, reflects itself in man's reality.**

We are the incarnate Soul, or a body, which has taken form as an immortal energy to experience joy. While on earth, we are meant to live in sustained ecstasy to free the ego and release the body. Man is distinguished in the earth's kingdom as the leader. We were made in the image of God, and as God's mortal image on earth, we are divine shadows or reflections, and we stand above all other species on earth. Through ecstasy and spiritual drunkenness, we are exalted to be able to transcend the physical world and contain the divine.

If we accept the view of many sacred scriptures, that man is created in the image of God, we are both corporal and spiritual beings. From one perspective, we are bound to the external world, and from another, we transcend it. In our wholeness, the universe is under our dominion and placed in our care.

By taking form on earth and becoming aware of the dimensions of our existence as soul, spirit, and body, we are able to become conscious agents in creation with the creator. It is consciousness that distinguishes us from all other species. Conscious love places us in intimacy with the Source of Creation and transforms our self-focus into compassion for all other species, filling us with divine grace.

# DĪVAN OF SHAMS: POEM NO. 215

*Behold*
*where I come from*
*and from where*
*the joy and sorrow of this world comes!*

*Behold where I come from*
*and from where*
*the suffering over the rain and gutter comes!*

*Why should I not return to my original place?*
*Behold where*
*my heart comes from*
*and from where*
*sightseeing in this dustbin comes!*

*Now that I don't have a mule*
*and I'm not a slave to one;*
*O dear one,*
*see where I come from*
*and from where*
*distress over packsaddle and manure comes!*

*You've gone a thousand years*
*past intelligence, illusion, and apparition.*
*See where you come from*
*and from where*
*the pressure of suspicion comes!*

*You are a bird with four wings*
*to soar toward the heavens!*
*Behold where you come from*
*and from where*
*the way to the roof and the ladder comes!*

*No one takes you,*
*and you don't take anyone for a goat.*

*See where you come from*
*and from where*
*the fear of herdsmen's commotion comes!*

*You hear thousands of cries*
*from the sky above like thunder;*
*you do nothing, and you don't want to realize*
*where these messages come from!*

*Since Adam was kicked out of Heaven*
*because of a snake,*
*behold where your safety*
*among snakes and scorpions comes from!*

*O heart! O heart, listen to me!*
*Reach far above the line!*
*Behold where the sky is*
*and where the line comes from!*

*Come to the gathering of the drunks*
*and lock the door from inside!*
*See where I come from*
*and from where*
*the vice and virtue comes!*

*Bring out the immature wine*
*and pour it for the mature.*
*See where I come from*
*and from where*
*the despair for every fool comes!*

*Don't be held captive;*
*your life has no border or shoreline.*
*You have divine attributes!*
*Behold from where*
*limits and expanse for the Divine comes!*

*Death breaks the cage but does not hurt the bird.*
*Behold where dying comes from*
*and from where*
*wings for the divine bird comes!*

*Be silent!*
*You've said enough,*
*and no one has discerned to know*
*where the noise comes from*
*and from where*
*all these assertions come!*

# SPIRITUAL ECSTASY

The word *Mast* in Farsi, translated into English as drunk, is an expression used in mystical poetry to describe a person who is in the state of mindless consciousness. It is a state in which the rational mind is disabled, but the body is still fully alert and functional. It is quite different from the description of a person who is drunk as the result of consuming alcoholic beverages and is not fully functioning, either physically or mentally.

A spiritual drunk is a person who is in the ecstatic condition of being completely dissolved in the love for the beloved. Mystics also speak of the heart being drunk, for in this state, the intuition of the lover is stronger than his knowledge or rational mind. All that the heart desires is to expand and to move toward a deeper intimacy.

> **If anyone asks about drunkenness, I answer that it is the loss of the ability to distinguish nonbeing from being, such as not being able to tell the hand from the foot. Being drunk does not mean to be incapable of differentiating between good and bad. One who is drunk with love is one who is in an ecstatic state of oneness and cannot tell himself apart from his beloved or the beloved from himself. One is drunk with wine, the other with the winegiver. The former is mortal, and the latter is divine.**
>
> Ansari

Rumi uses the concept of drunkenness as a metaphor to unite joy and the ecstasy of life with the divine gifts. It is certainly far removed from drinking alcohol in order to feel good for a while and having to face the consequences of the next day's after effects. It is notable to mention that the use of alcoholic beverages is forbidden in both Islamic and Sufi canons. If a Moslem gets caught for drunken behavior, he is to be publicly whipped up to a hundred lashes. This rule is still practiced in many Islamic countries and was very strict during Rumi's time.

> Learn about the secrets
> of love and drunkenness
> from me, not from the preacher!
> For I am the one
> who spends every night
> with the cup and the urn
> in the company of Venus and the Moon.
>
> Hafiz

Spiritual drunkenness is about the loss of the ego that imprisons the soul. Actions that are not in obedience to the ego are acts of drunkenness while in the ecstasy of love, and they are not limited to any extent by boundaries or measurement.

Drunkenness is the ecstasy of the soul resulting from the joy of being in the presence of the beloved and receiving the wine of love. This state is produced through bewilderment, delight, and through attentiveness of the lover in the presence of the beloved. It is a time when all senses and rationality give way to the creative power of love. This is a situation when the lover does not function in a logical way. It is called drunkenness simply because of the similarity to the condition of physical drunkenness and its effect on the behavior of the lover.

Drunkenness in mystical literature is a metaphor for the supreme ecstasy experienced when one truly yields to the power of love. It is the disorientation that comes with the surrendering of self-control to divine love.

> Make me so drunk that I forget that I am I!
> When I find myself ruined in the house of drunks,
> I will be free from the spell of life
> and from the duality of this world.
> When drunk, I will be standing on top of the world!
> Gratefully, I will sever my I from my I-ness
>
> Iraghi

Sufis use the term, mystical drunkenness, to describe the state of completely dissolving in God. It is the ecstasy felt when a person is aware of melting into the intimacy of communion. It is the moment when the heart of the seeker becomes filled with an interior awareness and is able to leave all attachments and worldly possessions behind. The most important step in ascending to a higher level of consciousness is the abandonment of physical attachments and letting go of being too focused on worldly pleasure, which is considered to be an obsession of those who are sober and bound to the physical world.

Spiritual ecstasy overwhelms thought and opinion long enough to allow the experience of living through the heart to replace all former mental orientation.

> *When sober,*
> *I am walking behind the lame.*
> *When drunk,*
> *I reach my love in one eager stride.*

Drunkenness, as Rumi describes, is a very positive reference to the ecstasy felt when the lover is moved by the energy of love of one person for the other.

The first stanza of the following poem begins with the predicament we find ourselves in when we are confused and don't know how to navigate in the state of spiritual ecstasy. We are invited to join the community of those in love and discover what it is like to be in a state of experiencing the joy of the soul! Literal descriptions or geographical locations lose their meaning, because home is wherever we are in union with the beloved!

# DIVAN OF SHAMS: POEM NO. 2309

I'm gone! You, too!
Who will take us home?
How many times have I told you
not to drink more than a cup or two!

No one is sober in this town!
One is worse than the other,
all mad, all frenzied.

Come to the house of drunks, dear one!
Come to where you feel
the joy of soul!
Soul has no joy without love.

Everyone is drunk,
hand in hand with others,
while the winegiver of life
passes around the royal urn!

You are endowed to live in the house of drunks!
Your earning is wine, and your spending is wine.
Keep the sober ones
away from this refuge!

Hey, gypsy lute player,
who is more drunk, you or I?
In front of a drunk like you,
my deeds are only a fable!

I left home; I met a drunk!
Hidden in every glance,
were hundreds
of houses and rose gardens.

Like a ship without an anchor,
he was flowing from side to side!

*Blind with envy,
were hundreds of thinkers and sages.*

*Where are you from? I asked.
He smiled and said, O dear one!
I'm half from the east,
and half from the west.*

*Half is water and mud;
half is heart and soul.
Half a precious pearl in the sea;
half is fixed ashore.*

*Be friendlier to me, I said,
I am so close to you!
Let me be,
I don't know close from far!*

*I have lost my heart and my rank.
I'm living in the house of drunks.
My chest is filled with words.
Shall I say them or not?*

*In the circle of the lame,
one has to act lame!
Don't you remember the advice
of the Prophet?*

*Such a venerable drunk
is not less than a wooden post,
for in its quietness,
even the Moaning Pillar wailed!\**

*O Shams of Tabriz!
Why do you run away from me,
now that you have started
a riot of this magnitude?*

* It is said that at the early days of Islam, there was a wooden post that Mohammad, the Chosen One, used to lean against while delivering his discourses in Medina. Later on when a pulpit was built for him, people heard a sound coming from the pillar. Therefore, it became known as the Moaning Pillar, longing for the presence of the Chosen One.

# THE WINEGIVER

The one who offers joy and the ecstasy of drunkenness is called *Saghi* (sometimes spelled *Saki*), which can be translated into English as the winegiver. This word is frequently used in mystical poetry with several different connotations. Sometimes, the winegiver refers to the heart, sometimes to divine power and other times the fountain of heaven. It also has been used as a metaphor for the spiritual leader or the perfect master.

> **Longing for the wine of love**
> **burned all my belongings,**
> **the day I saw**
> **the image of the winegiver**
> **in the shimmering flames of the wine.**
> Hafiz

One of the greatest practices of Sufis is to be detached from every physical bond. They become empty like a cup to be filled with the divine power that brings ecstasy from the hand of the glorious winegiver.

*Saghi*, or the winegiver, is the creative soul that makes a painter to paint, a musician to compose, and a poet to write poetry. The light of love and beauty spreading through the heart is the wine offered to everyone by the winegiver.

> **We are drunk with the wine that elates the soul.**
> **We are euphoric with the wine that clears the head.**
> **There are treasures in the heart of the winehouse.**
> **We are longing for the treasures of that heart.**
> Attar

When the divine winegiver fills us with the celestial wine, we dissolve and disappear, and we drop our veils claiming a new identity as the Truth of Love.

Anyone drunk with the ecstasy of love does not see the winegiver as separate from the self. Like a fish that is not separate from the water and unaware of

*The Winegiver*

the sea, the lover does not see love or the beloved apart from the self. The need for external rules and vows becomes unnecessary when this happens. Love turns into the guide and the energy that moves life.

> **Holding a bowl of wine in his hand,**
> **the winegiver was drunk**
> **as he entered the winehouse.**
> **All our vows were broken at once.**
> **Everyone cried out in ecstasy**
> **that all our troubles are resolved!**
> Iraghi

Rumi refers to the winegiver as the confidant of the soul of the drunks, the essence of transformation, and one who has the wisdom of acceptance. It is a name for a state of beingness and for the divine, who is the supreme ruler of all greatness.

> *O confidant of the soul of drunks,*
> *behold the thoughts and ecstasy of drunks!*
>
> *O monarch of greatness, by the light of your grace,*
> *come and enlighten the countenance of drunks!*

The relationship between the confidant of the soul and the one who is drunk works both ways. The light of love, poured by winegiver in the cup of the body, develops energy and offers constant creativity that is life-giving and sustaining.

Whenever we live freely in ecstasy, we give and receive life naturally. The contrary is also true, whenever we close our eyes to life or view it with a lack of enthusiasm or without hope, we feel the separation that causes pain and suffering. We experience a life that is not creative. The winegiver offers the lover the wine that produces a flow toward the beloved in a continuous cycle of releasing creative expression of love.

# DĪVAN OF SHAMS: POEM NO. 1382

*O winegiver of enlightened hearts!*
*Offer me the wine of your kindness,*
*for this is the reason*
*you have brought me here*
*from the desert of oblivion!*

*Pour it into my heart,*
*until I shred the veil and go beyond reason.*
*My spirit is consumed by judgment,*
*and my life is reduced by thoughts.*

*O heart! Don't speak of the beloved.*
*You are not even aware of love.*
*No grace of the beloved is in you,*
*even if your beauty rivals the moon.*

*The virtue of all sages*
*and joy of every wise man*
*have no ability or vision*
*to describe the beauty and aroma*
*of the rose garden of love.*

*The wine that turns to vinegar*
*never loses its sourness!*
*Seek not this earthly wine.*
*Look for the wine that*
*fills you with vision and longing.*

*O beautiful winegiver!*
*Pour me the wine that gives me insight.*
*Offer me the wine from the sea of love*
*and fill my heart with pearls.*

*Pour that precious wine
over the frozen cries of skeptics,
until their words become warm,
and their nays become yeas!*

*If I had no audience or critics,
my words would be inspired.
Offer me illumination,
or go away and leave me alone.*

*Like an eyesore,
you are glued to my vision.
O friend, turn the page,
or I will break my pen.*

*Anyone shouting has a hidden reason.
A banner carried on the road
means a king
or an army is behind it.*

*No kingdom remains barren.
Empty this body of your ego.
The soul is drunk in this water and mud.
Be careful not to slip and fall.*

*O Shams of Tabriz, O Light of Truth,
O graceful guide, gaze into me!
Save me, for you are the power that moves
and the remedy that cures.*

# MADNESS OF LOVE

The connection with the beloved develops completely through a condition beyond the lover's awareness. Mystics refer to it as the madness of love. The one who has given his heart to love lives in that madness, and he is not attached or controlled by any mortal lust or physical cravings.

> **Where is the beloved?**
> **Someone asked.**
> **In my heart, I said.**
> **Where is your heart?**
> **With the beloved, I said.**
> **And where is the beloved?**
> **In my heart!**
> Abu Saeed Abolkheir

The true lover is only in pursuit of what has captured his heart and has little or no interest in the exterior needs or wants of ordinary earthly attachments.

**Victory of love in the kingdom of the heart over dominion of the rational mind is considered the madness of love.**

Madness to Rumi is freedom from any kind of attachment. It is the victory of the champion of love in the kingdom of the heart over the ruler of the rational world. The one who tastes the true sweetness and joy of madness will never give in to soberness of the physical realm.

> *Madness is the vocation of lovers;*
> *silence is their product and asset.*
>
> *Madness of love prevents the lover*
> *from abusive and self-indulgent thought.*

The cynicism of the rational world is opposite of the madness of love. The one who is madly in love is one whose whole being is insightful and observant, even though the eyes might be closed to reason. The lover is capable of visualizing the divine command through the eyes of the soul while perceiving the beloved.

Madness develops a deep feeling in the heart of a lover and a sensation that grows into a guiding love. It urges one to do something special and meaningful in life. That feeling of purpose and meaning is the mission that has been embedded in the person even prior to birth. Once one assumes a physical form, human nature resists following a special mission. Personal reasons and the orientation of rationality could guide and align the person in a different direction. It works against a sense of mission rather than helping to accomplish it.

A mad lover loses all interest in this transient world to the point that even physical comforts become of little or no concern. Lovers lost in the beauty of love find material pleasures outside the realm of love to be pointless and sometimes painful. Once the bodily cravings are broken, and divine love becomes the experience, lovers do not wish to move in any other direction. It doesn't matter how much rational advice is given to anyone lost in the rapture of divine love; they are not influenced by it. There is little regard for the opinion of others, and there is an ultimate acceptance of the mindlessness, which is known as the madness of love.

> *No one's advice is useful to lovers,*
> *for love is not a flood that can be contained.*

A true lover is bold, truthful, and bright. Unafraid of dying or failure, the one who is deeply in love pursues the desire and commandment of the heart above all else.

The one taken over by the madness of love thinks only of the beloved and often seems to have little regard for the self. The way of true lovers is quite different from the way of those guided by their rational mind. Those who are guided by reason, seek approval, while lovers move fearlessly into dangerous waters.

> *The logical mind runs away from drowning.*
> *Lovers accept drowning*
> *in the sea as their destiny.*
> *The logical mind finds consolation*
> *in reaching a level of comfort in life.*
> *Lovers are focused beyond comfort.*

*Madness of Love*

Lovers will go through immeasurable pain to follow love, and yet they would never apologize for their direction or change their course. Their existence is nothing but love.

# DĪVĀN OF SHAMS: POEM NO. 2131

*Put aside your clever schemes!*
*O lover, be mindless! Become mad!*
*Dive into the heart of the flame!*
*Become fearless! Be a moth!*

*Turn away from the self*
*and tear down the house!*
*Come and dwell in the house of love!*
*Live with lovers! Be a lover!*

*Clean your chest from all hostility.*
*Wash it seven times.*
*Fill it with the wine of love!*
*Be a chalice for love! Be a chalice!*

*You must be all love*
*to be worthy of the beloved.*
*When going to the gathering of drunks,*
*become a drunk! Be a drunk!*

*The earring of the lovely ones*
*is intimate with beauty!*
*If you long for love's intimacy,*
*be a precious pearl! Be a pearl!*

*If your soul is lifted to heaven*
*when you hear this song,*
*dissolve in the melody of love.*
*Be a love song! Be a song!*

*Don't dread the darkness of denial.*
*Be the radiance of creative power.*
*Be the light! Be a haven of the spirit!*
*Be a haven of light! Be a haven!*

*Your thought takes a course
dragging you in its wake.
Move beyond thought!
Let your heart lead! Be a leader!*

*Passion and caprice
are locks leashing our hearts.
Become the key to the locks!
Open your heart! Be a key!*

*The light of the Chosen One
made a pillar moan!\**
*You are surely more than a post!
Yearn for love! Be the moaning!*

*Solomon tells us,\*\**
*to listen to the birds singing.
Don't be a trap to scare them away!
Be the nest for them! Be a nest!*

*When the grace of love is revealed,
be a mirror to reflect it.
When the beloved's hair is loosened,
brush it like a comb! Be a comb!*

*Don't move two-sided like a rook!
Don't travel bit by bit like a pawn!
Don't move every direction like a queen!
Be the master of the game! Be a master!*

*You gave away your vanity and wealth
to gain the approval of love!
Put those aside and give your self!
Be grateful for love! Be gratitude!*

*You were the four elements!*
*then became animal.*
*Now you are a lover!*
*Become all love! Be the beloved!*

*How long will you continue*
*to deliver words at the door?*
*Come in the house and close your mouth!*
*Remain quiet for a while! Be silent!*

\* See the footnote in chapter on Spiritual Ecstasy.

\*\* Reference to Solomon, the heir of King David, who is known to have had the capability to understand the language of the birds.

# BEYOND CONSCIOUSNESS

Spiritual drunkenness leads the seeker into the state of being beyond all concern about the physical reality of life and removed from any attachment to the ego self. It is a state in which the person moves beyond consciousness. The complete experience of love takes place in this condition.

> Give me drunkenness, so I forget about I.
> Ruin me, so I plunge into the house of ruin.
> Let me become free from life's trickery
> and relieved from world's duality.
> Dissolved into nothingness,
> I would rise above heaven.
> Deftly and fearlessly, I would demolish my ego.
> Why should I be stuck in the abyss of life's darkness?
> Why should I remain like a worm in a cocoon?
>
> Iraghi

Deeper spiritual implication is revealed to those who exist beyond consciousness and who allow the mystery to hold the fertile promise of the unknown and all that is yet to be created. In that state, one drinks the wine of truth from the divine hand. That is the ultimate blossoming of life and the experience of true freedom. The stark arrogance that presumes to know and see everything leads to duality and results in the separation of the self from the fullness of the heart. When a person is beyond consciousness, enraptured with life, only the beloved is fully and singularly in the mind and in the heart.

> *When you move beyond consciousness,*
> *you caress the beloved.*
> *When you move into the unknown, beyond everything,*
> *the beloved caresses you.*

True mystics or divine lovers are always living beyond consciousness. Yet, they still remain in an expanding state of becoming aware of the true self as well as unlimited creative power and capability that flows from love.

Generally, too much acquired knowledge or information, such as hearing about a world full of hazards and dangers, develops doubt about everything and can lead into fear and great sadness. The world could seem like a very unfriendly place if one is lost in the mundane details of every day. To become aware of divine kindness and generosity, we need to travel beyond consciousness into faith and trust in divine protection.

> **Lose your ego and dissolve into selflessness
> to find the revelations of the divine mysteries.
> Since the essence of existence is selfless,
> the mystery cannot be experienced
> through the conscious mind.**
> Attar

We only glimpse the experience of surrendering the ego and the awakening of our soul when we are in a state of altered consciousness and beyond the rational mind. That is when we are ready to enter the garden of the heart with absolute purity and eagerness and to experience love in its wholeness. We surrender and freely choose the path of love each and every time it happens, and we allow it to change us and make us new again. We run toward the mystery as a lover runs to the arms of the beloved.

The experience of being in the middle of nature as it unfolds in the beauty of spring, or of being completely affected and consumed by the energy of a work of art, can sometimes exalt and guide us to our ultimate freedom beyond the limitations of our ego-self and beyond physical consciousness.

Consciousness is the physical manifestation of the mind and the ego. One needs to ascend beyond consciousness to reach the highest level of freedom. Rumi considers the state of being beyond consciousness as living the essence or the deepest meaning of life.

Describing the mystery of the divine is not possible through a conscious mind. Making an attempt to articulate the mystery in ordinary words is an indication of arrogance and reveals a lack of discernment. Mystery yields to the soul that can be trusted to preserve its power.

> *Don't ask the conscious ones about the wine.*
> *Behold the glowing effect in the eyes of drunks.*

Beyond consciousness is quite different than being unconscious. Simply stumbling through life or being smugly conscious in a rational way is to delude yourself that you are in charge of anything. Yielding to the unknown feels as if life graciously flows through you. This movement is like tides receding in a mysterious rhythm between the earth and the moon and then rushing back to the shore.

Consciousness, as it is described in the *Divan of Shams,* focuses on nothing but the ego-self relying on rational knowledge; it is called a sin or grievous error. It is considered a lapse of faith for lovers. It is like the act of trying to steal the transforming fire from the divine hand.

> *Pour the pure wine*
> *to remove the self from me.*
> *In our faith, the greatest sin*
> *is to be controlled by the ego.*

Going beyond consciousness is to surrender to the generous flow of life. Focusing on the self would cause the beloved to hide behind a veil, delaying and preventing true union. Moving beyond consciousness leads to the suspended moment in time when the beloved caresses the lover and everything dissolves into oneness through love. That is when the deeper mysteries are revealed to the heart in unspoken beauty.

When a lover disappears into the light of love, the way the moon and the stars disappear into the rising sun, it feels as if one is wearing an armor of light, becoming free to go anywhere, to be anything, and to do everything without fear! The seeds of love germinate and sprout inside the heart and bloom into unlimited creative expression!

# DIVAN OF SHAMS: POEM NO. 32

*When you are conscious,*
*love pierces your heart like a thorn.*
*When you are beyond consciousness,*
*the beloved dissolves within you.*

*When you are conscious,*
*you are a prey for a mosquito.*
*When you are beyond consciousness,*
*even a large elephant could be your prey.*

*When you are conscious,*
*a cloud of sadness surrounds you.*
*When you are beyond consciousness,*
*the moon rests in your arms.*

*When you are conscious,*
*the beloved moves out of your reach.*
*When you are beyond consciousness,*
*the ecstasy of love moves your way.*

*When you are conscious,*
*you are depressed like a leaf in autumn.*
*When you are beyond consciousness,*
*winter would feel like spring.*

*All your wavering*
*is due to your longing for stability.*
*Accept instability*
*so you would become stable.*

*All your indigestion*
*is due to wanting to devour everything.*
*If you give up consuming everything,*
*even poison becomes a cure.*

*All your failures
are due to greed for success.
Surrender ambition and witness
victory flowing your way.*

*Accept the refusal of the beloved,
don't plead for affection.
Witness how the beloved
freely comes your way.*

*When the king of the east,
Shams of Tabriz arrives,
the moon and stars
dissolve in the light of love.*

# THOUGHT AND RATIONALITY

Thought is the alignment and integration of what is already known in order to reach for the unknown. Rationality is the process of mind allowing the use of logical or quantitative relationship to deal with everything in accordance with one's goals and plans. Manipulation of information in making decisions is processed through thought. It is a rational mixing and matching of concepts, ideas, and experiences, which allows the judging of new information against what is already known.

The other extreme of rational thinking is what comes through the heart combining divine intellect with feeling, desire, intuition and hope. This is considered irrational or hopeful thinking.

Most mystics believe that knowledge is obtained primarily through the senses rather than through rationality and thought. Thought becomes valuable when it deals with the heart, with mystery, and with its development.

> The thought of the wayfarer is the guide for the way.
> It is the thought evolving from the mantra.
> Repetition and hearing develops this thought.
> It offers hundreds of thousands of new meanings.
> The thought formed from delusion and logic
> is not creative, for it evolves from knowledge.
> Skeptics are those having logical thought.
> The thought that evolves from the heart is valuable.
> The thought that guides the way of the wayfarer
> is not from logic, but from the heart.
> Attar

Thought in mystical terms is a movement of energy in two possible directions either positive or negative. Positive direction of thought activates a flowering of the soul and blooms in ecstasy, while negative direction of thought smolders in the soul and leaves it in desolation.

> O brother, you are formed by your thoughts.
> The rest of you is made of roots and bones.
> If your thought blossoms like roses, you become a rose garden.
> If it grows like thorns, you will be burned in fire.
>
> Rumi's Masnavi

When thought is only mental or intellectual, it deals with analyzing and evaluating what has been gathered as information. It is like a cross-examination of all the evidence, and it uses reason to form a judgment based on the facts.

When thought is initiated and expressed from the heart, it offers unique ideas and creativity. The result is originality and a higher capability. Some mystics recognize it as divine intervention. Some people simply describe it as talent.

The whole realm of creativity is outside the process of rational thinking. Creativity comes from a source beyond reason. It is the connection with the source that links everything together. We cannot find the essence of anything by simply looking at the physical manifestation.

**If you want to know the source of the images appearing, look in the direction from which everything flows.**

Rational thought is powerless in front of love. Thought which stands in the way of love is scandalous and disgraceful, and it is an affront to the sacredness of life. Love does not recognize or acknowledge such thought. Rumi sees rational and self-righteous thought as being like a cane that is used only by those who are blind or handicapped. It is a deceitful imitation of the light luring us in the wrong direction.

> *Love is without reason; rationality is like a cane.*
> *Judgment needs a cane, because it is blind.*
> *When love arrives, thought dies in its shadow.*
> *Love is the sunrise,*
> *while thought is only a flashing light.*

Reason is the major way we determine the direction of our lives and how we make our choices. It is also the primary source of instability in our existence in this world. In a way, it is our rationality and our constant thinking that reveals the false side of things and presents them as if they were real.

**It is the heart and not the rational mind that reveals what is truly real.**

The rational mind sends out a disruption, not unlike the static on a radio, interfering and working against what the heart is trying to express and communicate. It disturbs the ability to hear and receive the messages of the heart clearly. The rational mind and the heart are both part of our body. Some of us benefit by these two existing side by side; some of us suffer as they stand against each other.

The body is like a tapestry. It is all interwoven, and the nature of how we live can sometimes be destructive and tear the organs apart. In reality, we are the ones tearing them apart by the way we live and choose. Who is the leader to guide us away from this? Who is the one we can trust to help us with this confusion? Ultimately, it is not our thoughts we can trust, and surprisingly, not even our hearts can guide us, because the opposing energy can tend to work one against the other.

**Our commander is found deep within our own essence. It is the one who is pushing and emerging from within that guides us to discover the truth. We return to the beginnings of our life, to innocence and pure love. Divine spirit never shows its face. It simply dwells within us.**

We tend to build our lives around what we think and believe. Rumi tells us to let go of our thoughts and not to hold them in our hearts. If we can keep the energy of life circulating and flowing through our hearts, we won't limit our capacity to love with the kind of narrow thinking that can harden us or turn our hearts cold.

We think about our lives, often searching to find ways to be free from pain, and we try to stop the bleeding from our wounds with ideas. Yet, it is our thinking that is the source of the pain. If we could let it go and release our dependence on thought as a solution, we might discover the gift of oneness through our hearts and realize the gift of joy it brings.

# DĪVĀN OF SHAMS: POEM NO. 1122

*Let go of thought!*
*Don't take it into your heart!*
*You are naked,*
*and thought is like ice.*

*You use thought to seek*
*release from suffering and pain,*
*not aware that thought is*
*the cause of your suffering and pain.*

*The realm of creation*
*is outside the scope of thought.*
*O foolish one,*
*see the opus, and behold the beauty.*

*Look in the direction*
*from which the images flow.*
*See the brook*
*that causes the wheel to turn.*

*There is a beautiful source*
*that gives such loveliness to the heart ravishers.*
*There is a hidden insurgent*
*that turns the face of lovers pale.*

*Hundreds of birds fly in joy*
*from the unknown in every moment.*
*At the same time, hundreds of arrows*
*shoot from a bow in their direction.*

*Without a reason or a cause,*
*beyond all principle and logic,*
*the baker works invisibly*
*to knead the dough without using hands.*

*Without the fire of the oven,*
*every heart and every stomach is satisfied!*
*The bread is offered in the market,*
*but the baker is unseen.*

*An infinite variety of images*
*sprout from the surface of the earth!*
*It is the longing of the mother*
*that turns blood to milk for the infant.*

*In the darkness,*
*a voice cries to God for help,*
*O needy one,*
*open your basket to receive the gift!*

*When the gift is too heavy,*
*it tears up the basket!*
*O lowly one,*
*no meal comes freely from the kitchen of God.*

*The one who fed the Israelites*
*from the sky,*
*the one who pulled the camel*
*out of the crack in the mountain,*
*the one who makes a hero*
*from a drop of sperm,*
*and the one who clears*
*the way for flight in a dream,*
*creates a form every moment*
*in the world of mystery*
*to be placed*
*as new creations along the path.*

*I have been ruled to become silent now.*
*One day, the ultimate reigning monarch*
*will tell the rest,*
*in a different way.*

# PATH OF GLORY

Love is the entry into mystery, and longing is the entry into the kingdom of love. The two are intimately connected with each other. The path of glory is the way toward encountering the beloved. We are bewildered in the desert of life to find clues that become our guide in the path of glory. It is like passing through the valley of the heart to find the source of the heartbeat in a comprehensible form.

**The path of glory is the mystics' way of searching for the invisible God, rather than responding to a God that is revealed in everything.**

The first step in that direction is to have faith in something more than what seems credible in the rational mind. The wayfarer has to reach beyond what ensnares humankind in the process of dealing with the issues of mere survival.

Along the path of glory, one needs to live beyond the desire to be in control, and surrender to the way of the heart. Cues and the guidelines pointing toward the next level of development appear only when the seeker surrenders. The footprints of the mystics are clearly seen and felt in their descriptions of being drowned in the sea of love. The mystical sensory experience of joyous conduct such as singing and dancing provide the exaltation that surrendering creates in the heart. They become our guides in finding the path to a new way of being.

Spiritual knowledge evolves from faith. The evidence of invisible things and our intuitive awareness make us remain faithful through the journey. The storehouse for this spiritual knowledge is the divine intellect, which runs through the heart and is beyond the control of the ego-self and the rational mind.

> **O my son! It is you seeking yourself; otherwise, no one else has the interest to see you. It is your ego that adorns you in your own view. You have to break away from your ego and squeeze it in your hands until you have destroyed its power. You need to confront it and discover its connection with Absolute Reality, so it would not be concerned with the self or focus on the reactions of others.**
>
> Abu Saeed Abolkheir

The opposite side of divine intellect is personal knowledge, based on and derived from physical information identified with the material world. Relying merely on that knowledge could cause stagnation or delay in the path of glory. The cause of it is the reasoning of the mind and mental evaluations that develop doubt. Rumi places human intellect far below the divine intellect. He says the only valuable knowledge to show the direction on the path of glory is what remains free from human logic.

*Let go of thought!*
*Don't take it into your heart!*
*You are naked,*
*and thoughts bring such severe cold.*

*You use thoughts to seek*
*release from suffering and pain.*
*Yet, thought is the cause of*
*all your suffering and pain.*

In the *Divan of Shams*, human knowledge and reason is analogous with apathy and boredom. Over-analyzing everything and trying too hard to get the approval of others causes repetition and eventually weariness, which could lead to disillusionment and cynicism. When in that state, the person becomes doubtful of even his personal capabilities. He loses faith in the unknown power and moves away from the direction of the path of glory.

Rumi reminds us that the human being is always in the spring of life surrounded by wonderful possibilities. Why choose a path that offers gloom? Love is the answer to realizing one's fortune and finding the path of glory, where greatness is found.

The human race is already linked to a chain of greatness. There is no need to twist and struggle trying to get out of it! Since everyone is united with everything in the chain, then we are all on a course that carries us in the flow of love. Lack of faith leads a person to struggle against the flow and to hold back out of fear of the unexpected. An invitation to share in the path of glory is constantly offered by love to us.

*I shall wash my heart of all knowledge;*
*I shall become heedless of the self.*
*One must not enter*
*the majesty of the beloved*
*as a master of all sorts of knowledge.*
*The heart of a mad person is aware*
*that life is only the shell of the soul.*
*To reach for such an awareness,*
*we go beyond knowledge*
*into a glorious madness.*

Thought, reason, and intellect all have both positive and negative effects. The lowest level of them is caused by our human intellect, which is connected with the personal ego. The highest level is the divine intellect, which is formed from divine energy and substance. Sufis strive to overcome the human intellect by seeking the clues and guidelines through the divine intellect. The ultimate goal of the journey is to find the divine intellect within the self and to find the ultimate joy and happiness as we come totally under the sway of our own divine nature.

*When the intellect began to describe madness,*
*the soul and the heart stuffed their ears*
*with cotton, not to hear*
*the tale of the two separate worlds.*

The Sufi master, Mansur al-Hallaj, taught the process of replacing human intellect with the divine intellect, and he identified himself with divine power. He taught that when man attains the level of self-annihilation, his human intellect is also annihilated, leaving the intellect behind. There cannot really be a lesser intellect through which man comes to know God, for everything is already the embodiment of the divine intellect.

During one of his discourses, Mansur claimed *Ana al-Haqh*, meaning I am the Truth, which was taken to mean that he was claiming to be God. As the result, the orthodox Muslims became apparently greatly displeased with him. He was flogged, publicly mutilated, hung on a gibbet and beheaded, and finally his body was burned.

*Every particle of your brilliance
is shouting, I am the truth!
On every corner, a being like Mansur
is hung on the gallows.*

Human intellect can only guide us, along the path of glory, to the doorway of God's sanctuary. Once we take a step across the threshold, it is love that moves us to transcend the intellect and surrender to continue the journey.

Surrendering to love is to let love guide us on the creative path toward being a lover. As a lover, we need to be aware that the power of freedom could somehow be threatening. With freedom, comes the responsibility of responding to all that are unleashed from it and the desire to share the fruits and creativity with others. Rumi calls those who can't see this and hold back, the weary ones. He believes we should close the door that leads to the path of those who hold back, as well as ending that resistance in ourselves.

**Being a lover is a lifelong journey along the path of glory. If there is no love, the path leads to nowhere. Dive into the flame and let it burn away all that is keeping you from being the best that you can be.**

If we develop insight into how love works to free us, it really can't touch or limit us in fearful ways. The divine intellect and enthusiasm will always go beyond what we can see or know, beyond our comprehension. Rumi taps into the awareness that the energy of love is the power behind all creation, and he draws on that power in order to be able to share and express it! We are only beginning to realize that love is truly what makes us free, for love is the path to glory.

# DĪVAN OF SHAMS: POEM NO. 638

All of the weary ones are gone.
Close the door of the house.
Let's all laugh at every thought
that brings about our disillusionment.

Ascend to heaven, for you are
descended from the Prophet.
Kiss the face of the moon,
for you stand on the crown of the world.

If the Prophet could split the moon,
why are you a cloud of gloom?
If he was so powerful and bright,
why do you choose to be so incompetent?*

O weary ones!
Why did you give up before
making a valiant effort to carve through
the mountain, like Farhad, for your love?**

If you are longing to caress the moon,
don't turn away from it!
If you are not ill,
why do you crawl under a blanket to hide?

It happened like that, or it will happen like this,
may not always be right!
Don't try to analyze who you think you are
or try to figure out what you're worth.

Why didn't you begin to flow
when you saw that fountain of grace?
Why are you still flattering yourself
after you have seen your true self?

You are in a quarry of sweets.

*Why do you look so sour?*
*You live in the spring of life.*
*Why are you withered inside?*

*Don't fight against yourself!*
*Don't flee from what could be your glory!*
*There is no need to escape*
*when you are already part of the chain!*

*You are enchained*
*with no way out.*
*Don't twist and turn and struggle*
*until resistance grinds you down!*

*Like a fearless moth,*
*dive into the flame.*
*Why be linked to your obsessions?*
*Why be entrapped in such chain?*

*Burn out in the flames,*
*until your heart and soul are enlightened.*
*Get out of the old carcass*
*and form yourself a new body.*

*Why are you afraid of a fox*
*when you descend from lions?*
*Why be a lame ass*
*when you have the strength of stallions?*

*The beloved you seek will arrive*
*to open the door to your fortune,*
*for love is the key*
*that opens all your locks.*

*Be silent!*
*Words are making you weary.*
*The one looking for you is*
*like a parrot in search of sweetness.*

*Poem No. 638*

\* A reference to the miracle of the splitting of the moon by the Prophet Mohammad. It was demonstrated before a certain gathering that persisted in the denial of Muhammad as a Divine Messenger. According to Hadith, one night in Mina, the Prophet split the moon into two by a gesture of his index finger. The halves of the moon appeared one behind the mountain and the other in front of it.

\*\* Farhad was an eminent sculptor, who was in love with a beautiful Princess Shirin, who was also loved by King Khosro of Persia. To remove Farhad from his court, the King required him to cut a channel for a river through the lofty mountain of Bisotoun and to decorate it with sculpture. Farhad was promised that if he could accomplish this stupendous task, he would receive Shirin as his bride. The enamored artist accepted the work on the King's condition. It is known that every time he would strike the rock, he called the name of Shirin. When the work was finally done, the King sent Farhad a message informing him of Shirin's death. Upon hearing this, the sculptor threw himself down the side of the mountain and died. Khosro lived with Shirin until he was assassinated. Shirin killed herself and joined her lovers.

# TRAVELING BEYOND

The development and growth of those who have found the path of glory results in an acceleration of energy and a greater expression of what is happening within them. It requires a transformation and change allowing life to be expanded in newer and more creative ways. When in the flow of creation, one's heart opens eagerly to the deeper revelations of the universe.

Traveling this path of transformation requires breaking away from routines and from the repetition in life, and it calls us to be more flexible and open to our creative power. We need to be free to move in a new direction looking for clues that would lead to discoveries.

> To reach your inner depth,
> you need to embark on a creative journey.
> Once you have attained that level,
> you will find your spirit soaring
> beyond the angels.
> You can only reach that magnificence
> when you travel within.
> Attar

When a disciple or seeker has gone through training with a master, usually before his final phase of preparation, he needs to break away from the master's presence and travel out of the area of his influence, so that he will be completely open for the final guidance of the master. The reason for doing this is to break the patterns that lock him into a certain way of thinking or a set way of doing things. This helps make him receptive to developing a more enlightened perspective.

> Always remain on the journey;
> do not stop even for a moment.
> Traveling makes your spirit divine.
> If you stop on the path for even an hour,
> you'll discover you have moved away
> from hundreds of possibilities.
> Attar

If the seeker is fully satisfied or becomes too content with whatever he has found, the movement of the flow slows down. The acceleration is reduced by the seeker's satisfaction. It is vitally important to contemplate along the way and consider what is missing on the journey. During the period of contemplation on the path, the seeker has an opportunity to recognize all that is missing. This will lead to the development of longing and an increasing urge for the seeker to continue the journey with a new wave of enthusiasm.

**Journeying on the path of transformation can be physical, where one travels outside his usual domain. It can also be spiritual to travel within the mind and the psyche in order to change certain habits or previously established behaviors. It always involves accepting new conditions, being flexible, and becoming aware of what will lead to the higher growth in the person.**

If the movement stops in life, the growth stops. Change is the essence of the flow, and its occurrence is inevitable. The wayfarer has to surrender to the flow in the same way a drop of water surrenders to the river as it flows toward the sea. Water that is trapped with no outlet becomes a dead sea. In the same way that the heart keeps beating and pumping a flow of blood through the veins, the rhythm of life calls for continuing growth. The alternative to this flow and movement is to begin the process of dying.

Moving away from what is already known and moving toward the mysterious unknown helps create the possibility of finding a new direction in life. It is the true source of all creation and discovery.

Shams of Tabriz was usually traveling from place to place. He never chose to stay in one place for too long. They called him *Shams e parandeh* or flying Shams. He believed that true traveling begins with discovering the self, and it culminates in losing the self. The best journey for anyone is to move away from the physical world and toward the interior world in a direction that follows a deeper and more hidden path within.

**Journey of the spirit that is moving in the direction of its origin is the usual path the seeker is led to discover.**

Even though the wayfarer is initially captivated by an attraction, as he moves forward, he has to face many obstacles and challenges that are encountered along the way. Those challenges, that seem unfair at times, help to develop the process for the seeker to become aware of his own capabilities and to recognize what is valuable and what is not valuable for his journey. Sometimes, the seeker is attracted in a way that seems to be a wrong direction at the time. This is an important part of the process of preparing the seeker to be ready to guide and lead those who will follow him one day.

Razi

Moving away from what is familiar and traveling toward the unknown possibilities, or toward a dream that seems impossible, is true freedom. The only way to take this journey is through the heart by utilizing the energy that stems from the power of love. The way of the heart has certain unique conditions that are positive in nature, even though they might seem negative in the beginning. The heart is aware of the need for accepting the liberation from this world as well as the next.

> *Liberation from attachments of the two worlds*
> *is part of the process of creation on the path.*
> *Letting go of material benefits is to profit in love.*

There is a deep attraction toward growth and expansion within every person. Rumi encourages us to take time to discover the attraction, give it attention and focus, following it with dedication and passion.

# DİVAN OF SHAMS: POEM NO. 214

*If a tree could move
from one place to another,
it would not suffer the pain of the saw
or the oppressive wounds.*

*If the sun and the moon
stood still like rocks,
they could not offer brilliance.*

*How bitter the taste of water would be
if the river stopped its flow
remaining still like seawater.*

*Air not circulating inside a well
becomes toxic.
See how harmful even air becomes
when it stops moving.*

*When the seawater rises
to become a cloud,
it loses its bitterness
and pours the rain of sweetness.*

*When the flame stops moving,
the fire loses its glow.
It dies out
and turns into ashes.*

*Look how Joseph of Canaan
moved away from his father's arms,
journeyed to Egypt,
and gained such prominence!*

*Look at Moses, the son of Emran,*
*moving away from his mother's arms,*
*he journeyed across the desert to Midian*
*to lead his people to freedom.*

*Look at Jesus, the son of Mary,*
*as he traveled from place to place,*
*he resurrected the dead*
*like the Water of Life.*

*Look at Mohammad the Prophet!*
*He left Mecca,*
*came back with an army*
*to conquer and rule the city.*

*On the night of his ascension,*
*the Prophet rode Borak, the winged horse,*
*to reach the pinnacle*
*of encounter with God.*

*If you wouldn't get tired,*
*I could count one by one*
*in multiple numbers,*
*many who moved away to success.*

*I have given you only a few examples.*
*You can figure out the rest.*
*Break away from the self*
*and enter the Kingdom of Love.*

# SONG OF FREEDOM

*Shelter is found in solitude, freedom is found in the elimination of worldly ambition, and friendship is found in not having any inclination.*

Aflaki

Freedom to the mystics is to be delivered from any limitation and restriction imposed by thought, action or effect upon the expansion of love.

**Free are those who are not enslaved to their own wants.**

The journey to freedom calls on the deepest desire to yield and to give up one's search for self-satisfaction. That desire leads to a more meaningful life as we become freed to discover the excitement and joy of love. Freedom develops an expansiveness of spirit that moves us beyond the typical worldly pleasures that usually replace love.

Rumi describes freedom as what can be found in the arms of love. Such freedom offers constant renewal and opens doors to the infinite possibilities in life. It is a freedom that develops in the awakening and opening of the heart.

*When I drink wine from the hand of love,*
*I am liberated and free.*
*When I kiss the ground of love,*
*I soar beyond heaven.*

We tend to build prison walls around our own lives when we remain slaves to all that we think we must have to be happy. That thought and focus can become an obstacle to growth preventing our experiencing true creative expression.

*Look at me,*
*I am free from thousands of restrictions,*
*for my heart and my soul*
*have become maiden and servant to love.*

The animals' life offers a certain freedom in their choices of where to go and deciding what to do. When the choice is between eating and not eating, the animal makes the choice to eat. The animal does not have to feel love in order to do this; it is a question of survival and instinct at that basic level of life.

**Freedom to choose to work, or to play, or to develop relationship is a process that may lead a person to love, but it is not love in itself. The reason is that those choices are all about doing something rather than becoming the essence of love.**

When we embrace life fully, we discover the real joy and the sweetness of it. As we open our hearts to others and see ourselves in their struggles and concerns, we discover our oneness with them. Freedom moves us beyond the boundaries, beyond our own self-focus, beyond our desire to control others, and it leads us by the hand into the openness of love. Freedom offers the possibility of creating heaven on earth by allowing pure love to guide us to express it in our lives through grace.

# DİVAN OF SHAMS: POEM NO. 1710

*When I gaze at your beauty,*
*I am free of wishing*
*for roses and rose gardens!*
*When I look into your eyes,*
*I am free of wishing*
*for wine and wine sellers!*
*I have pawned my house*
*to live in your ecstasy!*
*I have flattened my store*
*to be free from dealing!*

*I*
*AM*
*FREE!*

*Love has ravaged all that I had!*
*I am free from concern for profit or loss,*
*or from doing any business at all!*

*Talking about love*
*and stressing over credit?*
*I have accepted disgrace.*
*Now, I don't care about shame!*

*How dare grief mention my name!*
*I am dancing, dissolved in joy!*
*I am free from anyone's grief or sympathy!*

*I*
*AM*
*FREE!*

*Feeling bitter about what is too costly to buy?*
*Move on! Don't buy a thing!*
*I am freed from buying*
*or dealing with buyers!*

Without a doubt,
happiness and joy are embedded in my heart!
I am done with wishing,
or with regret for having too little or too much!

I
AM
FREE!

My reasoning is gone!
I have vanished into the wonder of oblivion!
I am freed of all reason and rank!
Now, I live in the splendor of love.

I boasted, and you denied!
I am freed from pretending or denying
 in this world or the other!

I
AM
FREE!

See the pack of wolves
fighting each other!
I did not descend from dogs!
I am freed from fighting over carcasses!

God knows the secrets of my heart,
and that's enough!
I am freed from gimmicks and lies
and free of con artists and hypocrites!

I
AM
FREE!

*I am freed from arguing,
Insisting, or repeating!
What I learned from love
will never be forgotten!*

*Whatever I plant that is invisible
will sprout and grow to become real!
I only plant the seed I want to sow!*

*I
AM
FREE!*

*The attraction of sharing with friends
draws out my words!
Otherwise, in this state of joy,
I am freed from needing to speak at all!*

*The radiance of the Light of Tabriz,
Shams Uddin,
has freed me from needing
the light of the sun.*

*I
AM
FREE!*

# DANCE OF FREEDOM

In the ancient Persian script called the *Avesta\**, the human being is referred to as *Aadam*, pronounced Ah dam, which was reflected in Christian texts as Adam. *Aadam* means I AM. *Aadam* is not only the first man, but he is every man.

**I AM THAT I AM** implies that I have not been made within a boundary of time. **I AM** indicates **I AM the Creation; I AM the Existence.**

The trust of this purity of being expresses belief in divine unity and love. Time refers only to the present. If one ignores it, it becomes past, and if one acknowledges it, it moves into the future.

> I Am That I Am is *Aadam*.
> I Am That I Am is pure existence.

**I Am That I Am** is the manifestation of the divine nature expressing itself in the formation of divine attributes in *Aadam*.

Man's life is the energy of love spiraling back to its limitlessness, moving with the universe toward an expanse of freedom. We feel the exhilaration of it when we come from the natural captivity of our bodies. Just like the particles caught in the sunlight, everything is dancing to the rhythm of creation in a similar manner as the electrons circulate inside an atom.

Our movement toward eternity is in the direction of lightness and purity. Mystics compare this exalting condition to alchemy, which is the process of turning copper into pure gold. This purity is the sperm of the lovemaking of existence, the seed that is in every heart, and the desire to become pure gold, a light in its joyful reflection. It is the movement of our soul uniting with its beloved.

> Love is the elixir of calamity,
> dissolving in dissolution
> and disappearing in annihilation.
> Become totally free of the self,
> for your heart is longing for this alchemy.

> **Die to your self,**
> **for you are yearning for love.**
> **You are longing**
> **to give birth to your beloved.**
> 
> Attar

Life cannot be stopped. It does not allow interruptions to stop the flow. Life is the essence of search, the essence of quest and the essence of moving and expanding.

Life is meant to be lived for the benefit of the development of love. It is the essence of **I Am That I Am**, of that which is uncreated and is in the process of being and becoming. It is not possible to separate being and becoming, for they are one. The present and the future are interconnected.

**Fear vanishes when we are able to accept that pain is also a part of joy.**

Since we are constantly in the process of being created and developed, we sometimes find ourselves in the dark fighting for our freedom. In that journey, we experience pain and sometimes depression. We struggle and resist the darker side of life.

**Rumi says if we take all the poison in the world, we need have no fear, because it will dissolve in the love that exists within us. Love is the energy that transforms everything and integrates it into our lives. Love is a magnificent and creative power, and we need to live that power to its fullness. Love in its purity is a manifestation of the divine expression flowing from the source of all creation. We can only surrender to the flow as it moves through us.**

---

\* Avesta is an ancient Persian scripture that was compiled over a period of several hundred years. The most known part of it is the *Gathas*, the hymns considered to have been revealed to Zoroaster, the prophet of Zoroastrians, who lived about 1000 B.C. in Persia.

Avesta was the first scripture to discuss the principles of heaven and hell, resurrection of the body, the judgment day, and the continuation of life through reunion of the soul and body. These principles later became the basics of faith for much of mankind, as it was borrowed by Judaism, Christianity and Islam. The original Avesta principles included twenty-two books, (historical, liturgical, medical and law oriented). It was fully available through the eighth century. Since then, much of the non-liturgical texts have been lost or destroyed.

# DIVAN OF SHAMS: POEM NO. 1554

*Like a particle,*
*we dance,*
*captured in the brilliance of your light.*

*Every dawn,*
*like the rising sun,*
*we radiate our light*
*from the horizon of Love.*

*We shine upon*
*oceans and the land*
*becoming neither wet nor dry!*

*We hear the moaning of copper*
*crying in despair,*
*O glorious light,*
*shine upon us; turn us to gold!*

*Responding to longing*
*and burning desire,*
*we appear as the universe and the stars.*

*To rest on the delicate breast of love,*
*we become a ringlet*
*in the necklace of the beloved.*

*We shred our earthly mantle into rags*
*to wear the majestic cloak*
*of the kingdom of love.*

*We are the dregs drinkers*
*on the path of poverty*
*now savoring*
*the intoxication from the grape wine.*

If all the poisons in the world
are poured in us,
they are dissolved
in the sweetness of our soul.

Even when the brave ones flee,
we remain heroes
in the heat of the battle.

We make wine
from the blood of the enemy.
Drinking it, we become
penetrating like a dagger.

We join the circle of drunken lovers,
as we become a ringlet
in the chain of love.

The King has declared our amnesty!
Why should we worry about
what happens in the other life?

Beyond the celestial realm
and the invisible world,
we reside above
the green dome of heaven.

Although we are veiled in a body of flesh,
we manifest as soul
in the kingdom of Love.

Within the body,
the soul remains pure.
As we release our attachments,
the purity expands.

*Shams of Tabriz
is the soul of the Soul.
We will come into union
in the tower of eternity.*

# HOUSE OF RUIN

The Sufi practice is to reach the Truth or Perfection through love and devotion. The path is a spiritual one along which the seeker becomes developed as a perfect being arriving at the Truth. The practice takes place in what is known as *Kharabat*, the house of ruin. The teacher or the guide in the house of ruin is nothing but love.

Before entering the house of ruin, the seeker has identity. Upon entering, the seeker becomes indefinable and is faced with the obliteration and liberation of the body from its physical attachments.

> *A palace is worthless. Ruin the flesh!*
> *Treasures are found in the ruins!*
> *Don't you know that in the gatherings,*
> *drunks become cheerful when completely ruined?*

Many descriptions have been written in reference to the roots and meaning of the house of ruin. Some say, since drinking alcohol and having unconscious pleasure is forbidden in Islam, the title of "house of ruin" was used symbolically in reference to the place where wine sellers and the pleasure givers were doing business in secret. Others say that the descriptive phrase was given to the concealed pubs or taverns where one would go to drink wine and consequently would lose his reputation and honor. Mystics consider it to mean the annihilation of the physical obsessions and bodily habits.

The house of ruin is the divine school for the highest human training without taking instructions from any master or teacher. The only guide is pure love. After the seeker has journeyed the path of truth, he becomes a perfect being to arrive at the house of ruin without any kind of attachment to the physical world.

> We are libertines
> residing in the house of ruin.
> We are mad; we are drunk!
> What is there to hide?
> We are what we are.
>
> Saadi

Outside the house of ruin, the wayfarer is still definable, but once inside, all expression of self is transcended. Love charms us and lures us inside and drowns what is left of us. What remains is love.

> **The house of ruin is where all behavior, all individual expressions and character become fused with divine intimacy. The journey begins with the annihilation of any action, which is not directed toward the beloved. The wayfarer becomes a lover, who has put aside rational intentions, and is relieved from any duality or division between feelings and actions. The lover then allows everything to dissolve in divine intimacy and no longer connects or associates life with self or with the identity of others. The final entry to the house of ruin is when the wayfarer enters a pure state of being and is fully dissolved in divine essence.**
>
> Lahiji

The house of ruin is the place of complete unity. It is infinite and limitless. The residents of the house of ruin are in full intimacy with their beloved. They are drunk with the wine of truth.

> *O heart, do not go toward the house of ruin*
> *even if you are a dervish of this world.*
> *Everyone is dissolved in purity.*
> *There, I am afraid you'll be caught in your deficiency.*

The residents of the house of ruin are considered spiritual libertines. They are people who have surpassed all carnal laws and are unrestrained by worldly convention or morality.

**A spiritual libertine is the one who has pawned his ego to the world of mystery.**

Those in the house of ruin are not conscious of their state of being or non-being. They live in an implausible dream, free from the past or the future and are liberated from self-awareness.

*Stature in the house of ruin is for those*
*who are liberated*
*from needing stature, credit or honor.*

Sufis believe that one has to go through four stages to become a spiritual libertine and reside in the house of ruin.

- Stage one: **Emptiness**, which is to become free from all negative qualities and every passionate desire that originates from the connection with the self.

- Stage two: **Illumination**, which means to polish the heart and the soul, removing every stain caused by the attachment to the self.

- Stage three: **Embellishment**, which is the development of divine attributes within the self.

- Stage four: **Annihilation**, which is the elimination of any attachment within this limited physical existence.

Those who have been liberated from bodily attachments and have melted into the divine truth of love will never return to following arbitrary rules. They would not become practitioners of abstinence and self-discipline for the sake of belonging to a group.

**The one who has tasted the wine would never be satisfied with keeping only the cup.**

# DIVAN OF SHAMS: TARJI-BAND* NO. 25

*My heart has gone mad again,*
*yearning for love!*
*Mad is the one who has lost his heart*
*and longs for union with the beloved.*

*Drunk is the one*
*who is unaware of the self.*
*My heart is the seeker,*
*which is infinite and beyond measure.*

*In the ring of the divine Sultan,*
*I am the seal of the ring.*
*Inside the chalice,*
*I am the fragrance,*
*and the divine King is the taste.*

*I am not of dust or air.*
*I am not of fire or water.*
*I am from the Source,*
*where all these are united.*

*I am the Messiah of love,*
*transcended beyond heaven.*
*I am the Moses of drunkenness,*
*bewildered in the glory of God.*

*I am mad! I am drunk!*
*I have burst the veil of my soul.*
*I don't listen to advice!*
*No part of me needs guidance!*

*Why should I be a Sufi?*
*I am a libertine in the house of ruin!*
*Why should I drink from a cup?*
*No part of me needs a cup!*

*Why should I be a drop?*
*I am drowned in the sea of love!*
*Why should I be considered dead?*
*My soul and heart are alive!*

*The body sleeps in this dust bin,*
*and the soul goes to paradise.*
*I am left without a place*
*with this reed flute that moans!* **

*I've gone beyond the self.*
*I've soared beyond the limits of time.*
*I've traveled to eternity.*
*I've taken a strange form.*

\* Tarji-band is a combination of several ghazals of the same meter, each having a different rhyme. There are forty-four Tarji-bands, which includes about four percent of the verses found in the original *Divan of Shams*, printed in Tehran in 1957.

\*\* Reed flute is made from a hollowed sugar reed of a certain length with several finger holes. It is used often as a musical instrument by the Sufis during their chants and whirling dances. Rumi refers to it as a metaphor for the human body emptied of egoistic matters and ready to connect with the divine. In the *Masnavi* he says that the flute-maker blows in every hole in order to reach into the heart of the flute and to create a love that causes constant moaning resulting from the separation and longing for union.

# PINNACLE OF CREATION

In the Koran, God tells the angels about the creation of man, **I am locating on Earth a vicegerent in my own image**. Human beings are created as the pure image of God's attributes or as the form of God's meaning. Divine knowledge is placed in the human chest. Mystics believe the human being is the mirror of God.

> **Since man was the final being that was created, he is the fruit of the tree of life. Once he is endowed with divine wisdom, he is able to reach a level of perfection.**
>
> Nasafi

The purpose for life on earth is the development of human beings. Everything else is created to support it.

> *The highs and lows of the world are you.*
> *I don't know who you are,*
> *but everyone in existence is you.*

The human being is created for the realization of the divine attributes and divine essence, which appear only in human. The angels and all other creatures, even though they share the same degree of piety with man, man is still more outstanding than all other species, because he was chosen as the one to receive the divine Trust.

> **The universe could not bear**
> **the burden of divine Trust.**
> **They cast a lot in heaven**
> **and my name,**
> **the mad one, was drawn.**
>
> Hafiz

Man is the talisman of the universe. He holds a treasure in his chest. He is born from a ray of divine glory. Even though he is made of dust, he is the precious jewel of divine confidence. He is the trustee of the treasure of the Light of Truth and is prearranged to return to his original source. Man comes from the celestial kingdom where he had the freedom of a divine bird.

*I was the divine bird.*
*See how I became earthbound!*
*I did not see the trap!*
*Suddenly, I was caught in it!*

*I am beyond the four mothers.*
*I am even beyond the seven fathers.*
*I am a jewel mined from the divine quarry*
*transported here for a visit.*

Although evolved from nothingness, man sits on the throne of the divine kingdom. His heart is programmed to see and identify the truth. His true power is revealed only when he is physically or spiritually outside the shield of the body.

> **Whatever exists on earth or in space is created for a certain purpose, except for human beings, who are not formed for a fixed or pre-designed function. Each one of us is created to experience the gift of freedom of choice.**
>
> Eyn al Ghozat

Rumi refers to human breath as being the same breath that Christ breathed into a dead person to bring him back to life. It is like the spirit circles within us igniting the power of love that was always meant to be ours ever since we were created. We catch the air of Christ, and we breathe it in, and we let it circulate and mix with our own, and then we breathe it out. We have been created with the same great nature that was flowing through those who were called out to lead as far back as Abraham. All it takes is to truly believe in a love that places this faith in us.

**Rumi tells us to walk shoulder to shoulder with such greats as Solomon, Moses, Joseph, and Abraham. Conquer the army of the stars, ride the sun, and flow in its flowing fire. Flow in the divine mission that created the universe!**

This flow is about a love calling us out to become the best we can be and to let the divine power do the rest. Our thoughts manifest as the world around us and in what we become. If we could breathe the breath of Christ and have the faith like Abraham to walk through the flames, our calling would eventually find us and make itself known! What would it be like to spend our life on a mission of greatness like Moses, Abraham, or Solomon? Rumi's message is proclaiming that it is possible if we could only believe it. Here is a test of faith that offers great hope for anyone who might dare to step from their dreams into the reality of a great love.

Rumi's message is reverberating through the centuries to tell us to realize that as human beings, we are the light of the chosen one, the pinnacle of creation, and we need to believe it to benefit from all the possibilities that surround us.

# DĪVĀN OF SHAMS: POEM NO. 2840

*Don't make an idol out of the destitute,*
*for you are a very special one.*
*Don't sell your self for too little,*
*for you are worth more than life.*

*Raise your staff to part the sea,*
*for you are the Moses of time.*
*Split apart the face of the moon,*
*for you are the light of the Chosen One.*

*Break the urn of earthly goods,*
*for you are the Joseph of grace.*
*Breathe out like Christ,*
*for you are the breath of life.*

*Face the army of the enemy alone,*
*for you are the champion of times.*
*Break down the door to your treasures,*
*for you are the pinnacle of faith.*

*Take the ring from the demon,*
*for you have the power of Solomon.*
*Shine beyond the gathering of stars,*
*for you have the brilliance of the sun!*

*Step inside the fire like Abraham,*
*for you are the happy innocent.*
*Drink the water of existence,*
*for you are the Khedr of eternal life.*

*Move away from nonbelievers,*
*for you flow from the essence of purity.*
*Don't listen to foolish deception,*
*for you are the summit of greatness.*

*Your soul is immortal.*
*You are overflowing with ideas.*
*You belong to the Glorious One.*
*You have arrived here as a ray of God.*

*You are what is yet to be revealed.*
*You have seen nothing of your self.*

*Rise like the sun at dawn*
*and give birth to your Self!*

*What a shame you remain veiled!*
*Don't hide behind the clouds like the moon!*
*Drop your robes of disguise,*
*and reveal the splendor of your glory.*

*No mine has a ruby like you!*
*No world has a life like you,*
*for this is the diminishing world,*
*and you are the expanding soul.*

*You are the sword of the Lion of God,*
*and your body is like a sheath.*
*If the sheath breaks apart,*
*it should not break your heart.*

*Your soul is a falcon with tied feet.*
*Your body is the anchoring stone.*
*Use your claws to untie your feet,*
*and soar beyond every limit.*

*See how radiant pure gold becomes*
*when it enters the fire!*
*The precious nature of it is revealed*
*as the brilliance emerges in the flames.*

*O dear one, don't run away
from the heat of the fire!
What would happen if you risk it all
and take a step into the flame?*

*I swear to God it will not burn you.
Your face will glow like gold.
For you are descended from Abraham,
and you carry his mantle of faith.*

*Break out from beneath the earth
and rise above the tallest tree!
Soar to the summit of nearness,
for you are the noble falcon of the King.*

*Come out from inside the sheath,
for you are the tempered sword!
Come out of the darkened mine.
You are the ever-flowing fortune!*

*Spread the sweetness of your heart,
for you are a cane filled with sugar.
Play a glorious song,
for you are the reed flute of God.*

# ESSENCE OF LOVE

The mystics consider the essence of love as the source from which the entire existence originates. The heart is avidly longing to return to its place of origin, and that is how divine love develops.

**The essence of love is the source of divine enchantment and transformation.**

As the desire to reach for the essence of love expands, the heart of the lover feels the expansion of its own territory and the opening of the door to infinite possibilities.

> **What is separated from its essence**
> **longs to return to its source for reunion.**
> Rumi's Masnavi

Formed religious beliefs create many icons and establish many symbols of love. People often let the icons hold the power of their beliefs for them. Rumi is proclaiming the human heart is the living, moving, flowing icon providing the passage that leads to the essence of love. We can feel divine love only when we have assumed our connection with pure love.

> **If you are drowning in love, don't try to escape. If you are killed by love, don't go after revenge, for love is a blazing fire and a sea without a shore. Love is the oneness of the lover and the beloved. It is an endless tale and a pain without cure. Logic is baffled in rationalizing it, and the heart does not have capability to recognize it. Yet, love is the life of the heart. If the heart is silent, love tears it open and filters it from its adversaries. Love has the power to give life and to take it away.**
> Ansari

The beginning of union and the final abode of everything that exists is found in the essence of love, which is the source of purity and is free from all taint and tarnish of the physical world. It is placeless and timeless, and to return to it is to experience inexpressible joy and celebration.

All mystery and treasures of the known world are found in the essence of love. Love is the medium through which Rumi says, I was dead; I became alive. The heart receives love through kindness the way a child receives awareness in the cradle.

Only those drowned in the essence of love taste true freedom. They become free from every attachment even of life itself. Love is a divine power that attracts spirit to itself like a magnet. Love is so grand, so magnificent, and so glorious that nothing in existence can ever reach its pinnacle, for love is always expanding toward its source in eternity.

We feel the ecstasy of life when we are about to reach our highest glory. That is when we feel the incarnation of love in our soul. Spiritual drunkenness, bewilderment, and desire for love are all leading us toward the essence of love. Rumi describes the desire for love through the heart and beyond the rational world as *Sarmast*, to be head drunk. The beloved is always close to the lover, but the lover truly experiences the union with the beloved only when reasoning is finally quiet and the head is freed from thinking.

> **Love is a precious pearl;**
> **I am a diver,**
> **and the ocean is the winehouse.**
> **Head down, I dive in,**
> **not knowing where I will resurface.**
> Hafiz

The depth of love determines the level of greatness and the purity of the precious pearl that Hafiz writes about in his verses. If the flow of love stops with small preferences and ideas, the lover remains small. When the lover plunges into the ocean of love without a shore and surrenders to its vastness, he can reach the essence of love and fuse with the beloved. It is the joyfulness of the lover that attracts the beloved. When the lover is in ecstasy, the beloved draws near, the heart opens, and love becomes a celebration.

Purity is what transforms the physical world into heaven. It is about truthfulness. Everything is beautiful in purity, as expressed in the innocence of an open heart. How do we move in that direction? We discover it as we develop compassion for everything and everyone, including ourselves.

**Human integrity is found through love and the spirit of generosity.**

Within every heart, there is a hidden pearl called love. The beloved is hidden in the mystery of the essence of love. The creative source of all expression is the deep and sacred mystery from which we were formed. The process of creation is the pure joy and the awesome excitement of living a creative life rather than living as a byproduct of life, result of life, or as an object that has been created. It is the wholeness of creation itself that takes over and guides us far beyond mere methods or just the physical process of creating.

Infinite drops of love fall on earth from the source of love. The manna from heaven falls on the desert as it did for Moses. Only the daily bread will be the essence of love that continues creating into eternity. There are hundreds of voices leading us to the heart of existence through a trail of music, song, dance, and pure joy! When we see, feel, experience and are true to it, we set it free. In truth, it sets us free! The chalice is placed in the hands of lovers, for they are love's hands reaching through us.

# DĪVAN OF SHAMS: POEM NO. 1770

*Selfless and filled with ecstasy,*
*love comes to me at midnight.*
*I become fused with joy,*
*for I am now in the arms of love.*

*Filled with warmth and fervor,*
*love sings to me,*
*I am the light;*
*you are my reflection!*

*You fly with two wings;*
*I fly with no wings!*
*You take pleasure in this or that,*
*while the thrill I offer is unlimited!*

*Although I seem modest*
*in my true devotion,*
*what I give is high above*
*every other companion.*

*My bowl is full and will fill*
*more than a hundred cups like yours,*
*so everyone will be aware*
*that I am not of this world!*

*My urn is overflowing,*
*while all others are only half full.*
*My soul and my heart flourish,*
*while my body languishes.*

*My image cannot be seen*
*with worldly eyes,*
*for I am not from this world!*
*My kingdom is elsewhere!*

I am hidden in your heart,
and your heart is hidden within you!
I am the pearl concealed and placed
inside this shell and in all others!

If you drink a cup more than me,
I will drink two urns more than you.

If you climb to the top
of the mountain like an elk,
I will consume with one swallow
both the elk and the mountain!

When I run,
the moon cannot catch up with me.
When I jump,
I jump beyond the wheel of heaven.

When I reach for my armor,
a ray of sun
becomes a dagger in my hands.

If these verses seem dry to you,
it is because you have not
been flooded with the flowing
of the fountain from my heaven.

I am not blind,
but I have the power of alchemy,
that is why I gather every imitation coin.

Whether I am just a fragment or the whole,
I am perfect for the beloved as I am.
I will never be consumed by sorrow,
nor will I consume any sorrow.

# PURE LOVE

Life is like a dream in which we are guided by a deeper reality within us. There is a spiritual truth available to us that gives inner direction when we listen and cultivate our awareness and receptiveness of it.

> **God has placed a light of merit in the heart of every person to distinguish truth from falsehood. This is not the type of recognition found in books or formal learning.**
> Al Jurjani

Surrendering in divine love makes the lover pure, unselfish and forgiving. Love is what develops the courage to be awake and face whatever might be happening in life. It is comforting to know that there is a source of energy of love that is always available to us flowing through the universe. When we surrender to the flow, it guides us through the challenges of life to ultimately bring us joy and contentment.

> **Although old, weary-hearted, and fragile,**
> **every time I remember your face,**
> **I feel my youth again.**
> Hafiz

Enlightenment is not just an awakening of the mind. Awareness increases as love is purified. Pure love elevates and guides us into transformation.

Awareness comes through divine intellect, which transforms us to experience the love that is pure and unconditional. When love is pure, it seeks the liberation and freedom of everyone, because the purity of love is freedom itself!

While the path of wisdom and knowledge develops the subtleties of mystical philosophy, it is the purity of love that overflows through mystics with passionate poetry and ecstatic dance. It is the burning fire of pure love in their hearts that cultivates such unequal impressions. Otherwise, if it were only their knowledge that was relayed, we would be receiving nothing except stereotype information.

It is pure love that speaks to the heart, not the knowledge of love. It is the drunkenness of unadulterated love and devotion that pours out ecstatic poetry and not the passion for self-indulgence. Such love is far from romantic love that is comfortable and cozy. It is a raging fire in the heart that burns up the lover from the inside out and consumes the ego-self.

Pure love is not about delicious perfumes and sweet touch. It is about the burning away of the self until we become nothing but love embracing the purifying thrill of becoming divine.

> **Love is not a game.**
> **O heart, lose the head.**
> **The ball of love cannot be stroked**
> **with the club of passion.**
> Hafiz

Rumi advises us that we should never lose faith, and be aware that even in the depths of suffering, the capacity for divine love is already within us. What we need to realize is that pure love is a path and not the condition of our soul. The reason we often fail in such love is because we give up with the first discomfort from the pain of longing for love.

Pure love is not a feeling. It is the willingness of the person to open his heart to the pain of longing and the development of tolerance for the complete dissolution of the ego-self into divine love. Pure love does not separate evil from goodness. It turns evil into suffering and goodness into joy and separation into longing. Love becomes pure when there is no distinction between joy and suffering.

> *I am the one who created the soul*
> *and the one who gave it pain.*
> *Discern that the one who gives pain*
> *is also the one who offers the remedy.*

Rumi believes that pain of love is the guide to our spiritual development. It is that pain which offers the wings of desire to make us soar toward the beloved. Ego-self, on the other hand, does not want pure love because it brings suffering. To Rumi, suffering is the recognition of the Truth and is in fact what transforms and purifies it through the alchemy of the lover's heart. It is a fire that burns away all attachments until the person has become pure and capable of receiving the beloved.

> *Call pain a blessing;*
> *discover joy in suffering.*
> *Look for comfort, security, and deliverance*
> *in heartache.*

When the ego-self is completely eliminated through the process of suffering and the pain of the heart, and when the seeker has been purified through the house of ruin, the soul is reborn into the life of the divine and the will is brought to perfect surrender. The person has now arrived in the state of an open spirit where he has reached the true potential of giving and receiving the energy of pure love.

# DIVAN OF SHAMS: POEM NO. 2501

*If I had silver and gold,*
*I would not be short of companions!*
*If my love had no need for gold,*
*I would be longing no more.*

*O God! Free my love from all worldly passions*
*for the sake of the faithful.*

*If love were freed from passion,*
*nothing would be scarce for me!*

*O Love! If you want my presence,*
*and if you feel compassion for me,*
*don't focus on absence and regrets,*
*for fortune is written in my destiny.*

*O my beauty! You are filled with grace.*
*Give up looking so needy and poor!*
*When you are truly content,*
*the world becomes all fortune!*

*It is greed that makes our ego*
*separate from us!*
*If love were free of greed,*
*everything would be interconnected!*

*O beautiful one! Come and be like us!*
*Don't go looking for riches or wealth!*
*If Satan were to be like this,*
*he would be a king on a divine throne.*

*He would no longer be connected with evil.*
*He would bow before the dust.\**
*His agony would be all devotion.*
*His distress would be all glory.*

*How great is the fortune of contentment!*
*How wonderful is the mystery of selflessness!*
*If we were aware of the hidden secrets,*
*existence would turn into oblivion.*

*This world is naught, and we are nothing*
*but flowing images and dreams.*
*If one who is asleep were aware of his slumber,*
*he would not fear the terrors of the night.*

*One would see a phantom in sleep*
*and would think it is reality.*
*Once awakened from nightmares,*
*he would be comforted and free of illusions.*

*One sees the dungeon of grief,*
*the other sees the Garden of Eden.*
*Once they are awake, they would see*
*neither the dungeon nor the Garden.*

---

\* According to the Koran (pp. 11-18), After God created Adam, He said to the Angels, 'Bow down to Adam'. They bowed down except for Satan, who refused, claiming that, 'I am better than he, for I was created from fire, and Adam from dust.' Satan was thus disgraced and expelled from Heaven.

# Union with the Source

Love and creativity, two of the most outstanding qualities of the divine, originate from the heart. We love and we create through our heart, as we break away from the rational mind and submit to being swept away by our deep desire for expansion beyond the self. When this spiritual desire develops, we allow our entire physical, emotional, intellectual and imaginative power to follow our heart's command.

> **Desire is a fire that radiates from the flames of love. It is the guide that leads the heart to the kingdom of the beloved. When the outcry of the lover overflows into a river of love, the heart receives the water of life and begins to experience union.**
>
> Ansari

Desire to a Sufi is a powerful magnetic pull that draws the heart to travel outward, while at the same time it is attracted toward the heart. It becomes a self-sustaining cycle. The desire to learn and to expand is the motivation behind the power of creation and is part of the inherent makeup that drives man to reach beyond the ego-self.

Desire is far beyond joy or pleasure; it is a reach for the unknown. Desire is what draws the poetry, the painting or the music out of the heart in order to experience itself.

If desire draws on logic alone in its action as an intention of the mind, it could lead to an evil act. In such a condition, desire turns into a selfish and inwardly oriented act to satisfy the self. Only when the heart openly expands outwardly, it manifests divine qualities in its always-mindless state. Rumi sees desire as the divine wine that offers ecstasy.

> *Compassion is like a river of milk.*
> *Fervor is a river of sweetness.*
> *Life is like a river of water,*
> *and desire is the river of wine.*

The connection with the source of love takes place through the heart moving like a breath breathing in and out. When we breathe in, we breathe in beauty, and when we breathe out, we breathe out beauty. When we breathe in justice, we breathe out justice, for whatever we take in through the heart becomes a part of the rhythm of expression.

> The heart is like a highflying bird
> desiring to reach its beloved.
> It constantly accelerates along the way.*
> It flies with the wings of insight
> and soars away from the physical realm.
> It flies above the universe
> beyond soberness or drunkenness.
>
> Attar

The heart purifies everything spiritually the same way it does physically. Whatever we breathe in circulates through the bloodstream and becomes purified through beating of the heart. Likewise, when we breathe in love, we breathe love out. When we are in the fullness of life, the heart is not only our connection with the divine power, it becomes divine.

> *The heart tears through its veil of darkness*
> *and flies away beyond the skies.*
> *It soars back to heaven*
> *where it was once flying with the angels.*

Everything that deals with our development is centered through and connected with our heart. It expands from our inner being. We make the connection of the external to the internal as we experience the rhythm of the divine breathing cycle. The power of life comes flowing in and then expands outwardly, and we move with it. We cannot stop it, or hold on to it, or we would extinguish the life.

The heart holds the key to existence, to everything around us, and we hold the connection to the source of our lives as a divine gift.

**There is a door to every heart, through which the light of Truth illuminates inside and becomes our guiding light.**

The heart is the deepest level of self and the origin of consciousness. To the mystics, the heart is not only the physical heart, but it is also the spiritual and divine heart. Not only does it know the mysteries, it is also aware of the origin. A true understanding of these concepts can help to bring about a profound transformation within us. It happens as we become aware that the center of our gravity can pass from the mind connected with the brain to the deeper level of self within the heart.

There is a narrow passage, through which the ego-self can pass into the heart. That narrow passage has to do with the desire to grow, expand, to be flexible and open to change, which is necessary to access the divine power in us.

---

\* It is interesting that over eight centuries later, science discovers that the universe is constantly expanding and that it is accelerating as it expands. The insight of the mystics is such a testament to the divine that lifts us beyond time.

# DIVAN OF SHAMS: POEM NO. 898

*Where is my heart going, so drunk?*
*I cried.*
*Silence, said the King,*
*It is coming our way.*

*But you are with me!*
*I hear you from the inside.*
*How come my heart is moving*
*so fearlessly away from me?*

*The heart belongs to us.*
*It is our brave hero,*
*headed for battle*
*with its own intention!*

*Anywhere the heart goes,*
*fortune follows.*
*Say nothing;*
*let it go wherever it goes.*

*Sometimes like the sun,*
*it becomes the treasure of the earth.*
*Sometimes like the prayer of saints,*
*it ascends to heaven.*

*Sometimes from the bosom of the cloud,*
*it rains the milk of compassion.*
*Sometimes in the garden of the soul,*
*it wanders like the breeze.*

*Follow your heart*
*to discern the hidden mystery,*
*where roses bloom*
*and streams of devotion flow.*

*What gives form to the world
has no form of its own.
What creates all appearance
has no appearance of its own.*

*The heart is right,
even when it seems wrong.
The heart is kind,
even when it causes pain.
The heart is the opening
that lights up the house.
The body diminishes,
but the heart remains.*

*The heart has caused many battles.
It has spilled the blood of many kings.
The heart connects with everyone,
and yet always moves alone.*

*A heart affected
by the spell of God
will break open the bag
and fly away like a comet!*

*O heart! It is foolish
to hold on to the bag without you,
for the content is gone,
and life is spent looking for the thief.*

*What creates the spell? I ask.
The king smiles and says,
There is no spell!
It is just the name of God!*

*Yes, but the spell
is the mystery of God!
Your delightful spell
is what moves within divine order!*

*The one aware of the heart, always
ventures with heart and soul.
What you see on the outside
is the body veiling the heart.*

*What you hear
is the message from within
announcing that the carriage
is harboring the water of life.*

# SWEETNESS OF BLISS

*Haal* is a term that Sufis use to describe a state of being that comes to a person at different times during their spiritual development. This condition is considered the sweetness of bliss, which cannot be achieved through an individual's own efforts. After the soul has been purified from attachments to the material world, it begins receiving the flow of divine bliss. It generates new energy as well as higher expectations, which increase the desire in the heart of the person to continue the journey with a new hope.

> ***Haal* is a transitory condition that strikes the heart of a person like lightning and penetrates his whole being. It happens again and again until the person reaches the effortless state of being and is totally drawn by the beloved.**
> Ezz Uddin Kashani

A Sufi is not meant to live with the thoughts of the past, for he is usually in the state of *Haal* awaiting the bliss. Although this state is temporary, it is the sweetness of love that gives it permanence. Since receiving bliss is beyond an individual's control, it sometimes is wonderfully pleasant, and other times, it can be frightening and feel overwhelming, depending on the sensations that are felt in the heart.

If the person is not completely drunk with the presence of the beloved, he cannot enter the state of *Haal*. Since he becomes aware of the worldly conditions surrounding him, doubt enters his mind. Although the attraction of the beloved is strong, the possibility of facing the loss of everything leaves the lover confused.

When doubt enters the mind, a need arises for assurance of connection with the beloved. As doubt is felt in the heart, the person loses the ability to distinguish between pain and pleasure and loses the experience of the sweetness of bliss. In this state, he needs to become more relaxed, more content, and feel reassured. A strong sense of the divine presence has to fill the heart to remove the doubt and fear and bring surrender.

*Haal* to the Sufis is the indwelling of God. When they become aware and truly feel that presence, the face begins to glow and a special light appears in the eyes, for they have glimpsed something extremely beautiful within themselves. It is the culmination of a search, like coming home after a long journey.

*Haal* is a divine power that builds up in the very depth of the heart and connects the person to all that exists.

> **Haal is both a divine attraction and a kind of deprivation that is inherent in the mystery of God. It is the cause of pain as well as reverence. It is the human discovery of the mystifying rarities, which move like a rolling wave through the sea of existence. It is the gift of God to humanity and the foundation of the unfolding of the universe. It is the manifestation of the qualities of the divine. It arises from divine order and reveals the divine light.**
>
> Ruzbehan

Some strictly formed religious teachings prevent us from experiencing *Haal* and discourage the pleasurable excitement of ecstasy. They believe excessive joy and contentment are states that could cause us to fall short of God's purpose. Mystics see this point of view as a denial of joy and a refusal of the divine gifts from God. The sweetness of bliss is something precious that is meant to enrich our lives, and ultimately make us more loving to each other.

> *We eat heartily,*
> *for we are aware of the King's generosity.*
> *We surpass everyone in drinking,*
> *for we know we will always receive more.*
>
> *Ecstasy does not distract us*
> *from serving the King.*
> *Being fully drunk at this end,*
> *is not to fall short in the other.*

Although moments of *Haal* are short-lived, they can be transformative and have long lasting positive effects. By temporarily expanding the person's feelings and behavior, the sweetness of bliss supports and stimulates creative ideas, benevolent actions, and strengthens spiritual connections. Because *Haal* is a pleasant experience of living in bliss, almost anyone is drawn to repeat it, for it triggers an upward spiral leading to enhanced emotional, spiritual, and physical well-being.

Rumi tells us to seize life and delight in every pleasure. We are to relish and enjoy every day of our lives. Each day is God's gift to us, and we should make the most of every moment by savoring and receiving the joy in its fullness.

Living in joy produces our highest functioning, not only in the present, but over a long period of time. We need to cultivate positive emotions in ourselves and in those around us, not just as end-states in themselves, but as a means toward achieving spiritual growth and harmony.

# DĪVĀN OF SHAMS: POEM NO. 1987

*Now, I am only half drunk.*
*Be kind and pour me one more cup!*
*When in the company of grace,*
*don't bother with right and wrong.*

*Don't go looking for those who are crying*
*and shouting about injustice or cruelty.*
*Stop carrying guilt for others!*
*Lie back and tend to your own heart!*

*Be always drunk and live in bliss*
*with music and song on one hand,*
*and the beauty and charm*
*of your beloved on the other.*

*Don't let the sweet taste of love*
*turn into an illusion or a dream!*
*Like an insistent beggar,*
*seize what brings you divine sweetness.*

*Don't be a child who keeps whining*
*for more treats and candy!*
*Gather only what sweetens your taste for life*
*and fill your basket with it.*

*Go for that elusive sweetness*
*that is worth thousands of lives!*
*If you need to be jealous of something,*
*be jealous of that kind of greatness!*

*Once you find sweet love,*
*steal a tender kiss from those lips.*
*To reach intimacy with your beloved,*
*align with love, like an astrologer with a star.*

*When it is time for fasting,*
*don't bother to gather earthly bowls.*
*Receive your ecstasy and joy*
*from the divine bowl that lasts forever.*

*Dance with delight as if you are at a feast!*
*Always stay in the center of the circle*
*without attracting attention to yourself.*
*Seek the love that develops oneness!*

*When the blissful bride of soul*
*reaches the bridal chamber in joy,*
*feed her from the exalted table.*
*Shelter her under the canopy of devotion.*

*You have become weary of words*
*thinking no one is intimate with you.*
*Handle the mirror of speech tenderly*
*and wrap it inside velvet cushions!*

# COMFORT OF THE SOUL

The soul enters the body to enjoy and experience bliss. When the body can no longer offer satisfaction, the soul departs. The essence of the human being is his soul. It holds the awareness of everything from an overall perspective to the smallest detail. The soul has the consciousness of self and awareness that it has potential to expand forever.

**Life is the expression of energy into the body, and death is its return to infinite energy source. Spirit is the life of the body and is pure energy.**

The soul is the cause of unification and separation, downfall and redemption, anger and calmness. Satisfaction or frustration are both expressions of the soul that cause connection with others or separation from them. The soul of matter does not exist in such duality, because it does not have the awareness of itself. Consciousness opens the possibility of choice to the human soul. That awareness creates the opening to the divine nature.

Comfort of the soul is obtained when the soul is in the light of union, and its misery comes when it is in the darkness of separation. Love is the ultimate comfort that reconciles all the pain, suffering, bitterness and scarcity and makes the necessary transformation to become joy to the soul. Love can offer comfort to the soul even when the soul is experiencing the pain of separation.

Mystics believe the soul has five different characteristics:
- Emerging soul as the one in plants.
- Animal soul that is merely for existence.
- Ego soul that relates to individuality.
- Human soul that is aware of life.
- Celestial soul that is always pure.

The first three relate to the physical world; the last two relate to divine soul.

> **The soul expands beyond east and west.**
> **Wisdom and awareness are within the soul.**
> **Physical body is the expression of the soul.**
> **Dying is only the death of the body.**
> Rumi's Masnavi

In the *Divan of Shams*, Rumi considers the beloved as the Soul. The connection with the Soul is through the heart. The sacred flow between the two creates life and its meaning. When love becomes the silent flow of energy between them, it brings us comfort.

> *Be silent and open the window to your heart.*
> *That is a way of conversing with your soul.*

The soul carries divine love. Every organ of the body takes direction from it. The soul is the essence of greatness and splendor. When the soul becomes aware of the Truth, it would no longer have attachment to the body.

> *Come, O source of purity and light,*
> *O Shams of Tabriz.*
> *This soul filled with greatness and elegance,*
> *is frozen without you.*

The soul is the splendid field of heaven in which the heart and the mind are harvesters. Its development is achieved through reduction of the physical extravagance in our lives. The soul does not belong to either the physical world or the celestial realm. It exists everywhere, yet it is unseen by the eyes. After it leaves the body, it returns to the original meadow beyond what can be expressed, where it continues its joy.

# DIVAN OF SHAMS: POEM NO. 207

*When in pain,*
*you are the comfort of my soul,*
*and when I am in the bitterness of scarcity,*
*you are my ever flowing treasure.*

*I surrender into the flow*
*for you carry my soul*
*beyond the limits of imagination*
*and what reason can grasp.*

*Your generosity*
*allows me to gaze coyly into eternity.*
*O Lord! How could I ever be deceived*
*by mortal temptations?*

*The joyful sound of the one*
*who speaks your name,*
*even in my dream,*
*is greater than all the riches of the world.*

*O my Beloved!*
*The image of you in my prayer*
*is more essential and binding*
*than all those uttered verses.*

*You are the compassion and mercy*
*in the sin of the infidels.*
*Even the cruelty*
*in the rulers and leaders is in you.*

*If the Infinite Bounty,*
*offers me every kingdom*
*and lays the universe at my feet,*
*you are still my hidden treasure.*

*I would surrender my soul,*
*and kiss the ground in gratitude,*
*for among all of these riches,*
*I would only choose your love.*

*Living in eternity means a moment*
*of being held in your arms.*
*It is only in that union*
*when time stops forever for me.*

*Life is a container,*
*and union with you is the sweetness in it.*
*What is the use of a container without you?*
*It is only the burden of carrying a load.*

*There was a time when I had*
*thousands of passionate dreams.*
*I lost them all*
*in my desire to be in your arms.*

*I have become secure*
*through the support of your grace.*
*I hear the proclamation within,*
*you are the soul of the world!*

*My heart and soul are filled*
*with the splendor of your essence.*
*There is no other voice but yours,*
*even when I hear that everything is you.*

*You unite with my soul*
*even when my body is unaware.*
*Although separate from the body,*
*your image is revealed in me.*

*I have aged while longing for your love,*
*but when I hear Tabriz,*
*my youth returns to me.*

# MYSTERY OF THE ESSENCE

**The ultimate stage in life's journey is the evolution from the personal self to the true Self, to unite with the essence of being.**

We are created to be, to exist, to live, and to love. The gathering of material possessions or establishing a worldly identity does not contribute much to experiencing the fullness of life.

> **Relationship between the physical world and the spiritual world is the same way as life is to death. We have been placed temporarily here in transition and will not be totally forgotten for a long time. The same way that being here was not by our choice, when to leave this place is also not our decision. Know that anything we gather here is not suitable for the other world, which has its own properties. What is made here is only for spending here.**
> Sohrevardi

Our creation did not begin with a particular purpose in the mind of our creator except to create. Life continues for the sake of the continuation of life itself. It is the nature of creation to expand. When we speak of expanding in a certain direction, it is not necessarily to progress, nor is it to regress. Our expansion is to move toward the fullness of being, which is the realization of the true Self.

> **The expansion of the heart happens
> when the ego contracts;
> the contraction of the heart happens
> when the ego expands.**
> Bastami

To live is to be. It is the divine power that develops the expansion and the recognition of being. The power of creativity is revealed as the personal human self creates the divine Self. Rumi says to be is the best way of presenting the beloved as the beloved is presenting you.

*The sweetest sweetness is the feeling of becoming one with divinity itself.*

How does creative power expand? What makes creativity flow? When the power of creativity is creating itself, it is reaching for its fullness. When creation stops, everything freezes, and the flow is cut off. What is attractive and brings the greatest excitement in life is the energy that melts the ice to continue the creative flow.

**Being in the flow is generated and caused by our excitement and innate longing for wholeness. The energy of excitement expands creativity. Creativity pulls and draws out joy. We are created, and we create in order to generate joy.**

Whatever exists in this world is affected by love, because everything grows from love. The development and expansion of the arts happens through the energy of love. There is a zone of creativity that opens to love to express its fullness in music, painting, poetry, dance, and in all other creative expressions.

We learn to live in the enchantment and bewilderment by letting it create through us and within us. We grow into the awareness that we are living the beauty of heaven in our existence here on earth.

The ultimate goal and the purpose of life is to live its deepest meaning in the flow and in the fullest expression of oneness and communion with others.

Mystics observe three levels of development in the flow toward the full expression of oneness.

**The initial phase is dissolving** – It is when the beloved appears in a certain identifiable image or in a variety of forms. In this phase, the lover sees everything dissolving into the beloved.

**The second phase is transformation** - This happens when the image of the beloved appears to the lover through certain demeanors or characteristics. The lover in this phase sees every action as the manifestation of the beloved.

**The third phase is realization** - This happens when the beloved seems to appear everywhere, in everything and in everyone. In this ultimate phase, the lover recognizes that all existence is a manifestation and sign of the beloved. The lover identifies the beloved in every trait and behavior.

How do we allow the essence of beauty hidden in others to expand within us, to help us develop, and to come to know the beloved through embracing all existence in divine love? The transformation is set in motion by our surrendering to pure love that is beyond what can be described or controlled, and by allowing pure love to hold us in the mystery of the essence and energy of love.

# DIVAN OF SHAMS: POEM NO. 1458

*I can never leave you,*
*not for a moment, not for an hour.*
*You are in everything I do.*
*You are my everything.*

*My drink is your sweetness.*
*I move to your command.*
*I am a tired prey in your hands,*
*and you are my consuming lion.*

*Your soul and my soul*
*are truly One Soul.*
*I swear to our One Soul,*
*I long for no one but you.*

*In the garden of your grace,*
*I am only a germinating sprout.*
*The crown of my blooming*
*is the desire to be in your arms.*

*This world feels like a wall*
*of thorns surrounding you.*
*Every thorn that pierces my heart*
*becomes the scent of blossoming in your arms.*

*When thorns arouse such desire for being in your arms,*
*imagine the splendor of your rose garden.*
*The mystery of you surrounds my whole being*
*and takes away all my secrets.*

*Just like the sun that attends*
*the moon in the darkness of the sky,*
*I know that you will never leave me*
*alone in the gloom of this world.*

*Once a poor dervish prayed
for me to be granted God's providence,
as if such opportunity and gift
were granted only with a prayer.*

*I see the entire universe like images
formed by the steam above a bath.
Now that you have blown away the image of me,
I can only reach out in your direction.*

*Everyone breaks away from the chain
in the hope of finding his soul mate.
Tell me whose soul mate am I
enchained in this snare?*

*O my soul, you are circling
about my heart like a thief!
I know what you are looking for,
O lovely ravisher of my heart!*

*You are concealing fire
behind the veil of your disguise.
You are here to set my existence
and all my belongings ablaze.*

*You are my meadow and my garden!
You are the cure of my illness!
You are the Joseph of my vision!
You are the success of my endeavors!*

*You are circling around my heart!
I am circling around your door!
I flow freely in your hands
bewildered in the course of your compass.*

*If I ever tell a tale of sadness*
*in the presence of your charm,*
*I am not worthy of joy.*
*I swear to God I deserve to be grieved!*

*Everyone is dancing to the rhythm*
*played by the tambourine of destiny!*
*No one could dance without your beat!*
*No one could move unless you move!*

*The sound of the tambourine is hidden,*
*and yet the dance of life is visible!*
*What causes longing is a mystery,*
*no matter where the tingling is felt.*

*I will be silent in my zeal,*
*for you are like sugar cane,*
*and I am a cloud scattering sugar.*
*It is only your sweetness I rain.*

*I flow in the water; I swirl in the dust.*
*I glow in the fire, and I move in the air.*
*These elements circle around me,*
*yet I am not made from them.*

*Sometimes I am brave; sometimes I am fearful.*
*Sometimes I am light, and sometimes I am dark.*
*Because of the form you have given me,*
*sometimes I consent, and sometimes I deny.*

*Shams of my soul and heart*
*is always within the Truth of Tabriz.*
*Even though in the body's flesh,*
*I am troubled no more.*

# JOY OF ETERNAL LOVE

The urn is filled; its head is covered and sealed until the wine becomes pure and ready to pour out the drink of ecstasy. Abraham, the prophet of the Israelites and a sculptor of unlimited deities, walks through the fire at the command of the Pharaoh, and the fire turns into a garden of flowers.

When faith develops sufficient strength, it becomes the expression of the faithful. It then receives the grace of support offered through divine order.

Abraham goes through the experience of breaking all the deities he had sculpted for worship. Prior to entering the fire, he surrenders to God through his faith. Instead of burning in the fire because of being accused of sin, God appears as the provider and life giver watching over him. Faith is the longing of the believer and his total trust in God to respond with love.

> **Joyous is the heart that is aware**
> **of the sweetness of serving divine love**
> **and the comfort and pleasure**
> **of being in the arms of the beloved.**
> Ruzbehan

The love out of which we have been created is far greater than we could ever come to realize. We are being cared for and developed in a way that is much more affectionate and loving than we have been led to believe.

Mystics tell us that as human beings we are a power that is superior to any other aspect of the physical world. By means of the energy of the collective consciousness, we come to realize that joy is offered to us through a love that is truly eternal. The joy giver offers us abundance beyond any reason or rational explanation. The awareness that we are constantly guided to enjoy the sweetness of love is what brings us the sense of security.

> **What is joy?**
> **It is to get excited about the true dawn,**
> **and become blazing fire**
> **even before the sun rises.**
> Attar

A constant awareness of the presence of the divine joy giver within the heart is already embedded in the true nature of human beings. The recognition that we are created for pure joy is what removes doubt and fear. The feeling of longing, which is constantly with us, is because we are aware and remember the infinite joy that we experienced before our soul was formed into our body. After realizing that mortal life is not going to satisfy that desire, we turn within to our own inner power, and our lives become the expression of sharing the inner joy and exuberance with those around us.

> *You will be riding joy*
> *with the Sufis of pure belief*
> *only when you step outside*
> *the formal belief of the Sufis.*

Attachment to material possessions causes us to become frozen, much like the solid matter that we have accumulated around us. Like the urn, the mud around the seal of our own lives has to be removed to get to the pure wine inside. We need to allow the heat of love from within our hearts to melt the frost that we have developed around ourselves.

The pure power that creates always caresses the created with love and nurtures it to develop and expand. There is an implicit promise that the entire creation is sharing in the feast of love and is moving toward harmony. No matter what we believe, the one who loves is there to offer us joy in a way that we will know and recognize in our heart.

The difficulties we experience in life are usually caused because we are seeking satisfaction. When we become aware that the divine joy giver is regularly offering us that blissful state, it helps to heal our doubt and grief, and we awaken to the truth that we were created to be that joy.

# DĪVAN OF SHAMS: POEM NO. 1395

*I am the joy giver of eternal love.*
*My fingers play the song of ecstasy.*

*I comb the hair of bliss,*
*and I remove the hair of grief*
*until the soul becomes all enticing*
*to offer the fullness of joy.*

*I then remove the mud*
*from the top of the urn*
*to loosen the seal*
*and take away its sober head.*

*I am the heir to Abraham!*
*I am in love with every abode of fire!*
*I love the soul and the divine wisdom,*
*and I am a foe to all pretenders.*

*When life couples with the sun,*
*it is always springtime!*
*The blood in our hearts is boiling*
*to melt the frost of our bodies.*

*What makes the moon melt*
*its brilliance upon us?*
*It is the fire of longing in the heart,*
*and the love for the source of all beauty!*

*The power of love is attracting me.*
*It is pulling me by the ears.*
*The arrows of calamity fly toward my body*
*turning me into a protector and shield.*

*Although tossed between good and evil,*
*I am drowning in the sea of sweetness.*
*Even though I move from place to place,*
*I am always renewed by the scent of home.*

*I am created to dwell with the beloved.*
*I am coupled with divine grace.*
*Logic entered my mind*
*and tricked me into separation.*

*O my sweet speaking King!*
*As long as blood circulates in my veins,*
*I am walking, running or flying to you,*
*for I am moving toward home.*

*That eternal sweet scent of love,*
*and that ear pulling attraction*
*is turning me into flowing water*
*to tend the meadows and rose gardens.*

*Like the yearning Jacob,*
*I long for the return of my beloved.*
*The kindness of Joseph of the soul*
*has sent me this robe as a gift.*

*O Love, how truly joyful you are!*
*You are the archer holding the bow of loyalty.*
*No one in this world or the next*
*can equal you in grace.*

*Although I am not worthy,*
*I am held in the arms of the beloved.*
*I am carrying fragile glass*
*and throwing stones, for I am a glass breaker!*

When elephants march to attack
the House of God,
like the divine swallows,
I rush to the help of its defenders.

I am the polisher of every mirror.
I am the hero in the middle of the field.
I am the food for every hunger.
I am the star of every galaxy.

I am the meaning behind all stature and deed.
I am the reflection of eternal grace.
I am the kingdom of all good and evil.
I am the gardener of every garden and meadow.

If the fire is ill-natured,
its flames burn everything,
and when the fire is pleasing,
its grace spreads to every place.

Even if you see this as wrong,
you will still receive your share of the feast,
for I am the reflection of the divine justice,
and I create everything in harmony.

O king of kings, it is time for you!
O master of universal grace,
speak with generosity
what my lips cannot pronounce!

# CONNECTING WITH THE SOUL

When a call is heard from within, it is usually a call for union, not for separation. The Sufi expression of *Fana*, or annihilation, is usually followed by *Bagha*, which means moving toward the Beloved.

> **Connecting with the Beloved takes place after the lover has eliminated all attachment to the ego and has attained an utterly pure spirit. When the darkness has vanished, and the light has risen in the sky of the heart, the person attains the brightness of the sun or of many suns. The heart becomes all light. The subtle body becomes light. The material veil becomes light. The person becomes endowed with divine virtues and attributes. The senses, such as the hearing and sight, the hands, the whole exterior and interior of the lover, all become light.**
>
> Razi

*Bagha* is the path through which spirits intersect and connect to the flow of creation when true union is felt. The human soul is not separated from it, which is why everyone is drawn into spiritual growth in life. It is the heightened moment when one becomes fully renewed and falls into divine union.

The Source of the Divine is constantly creating, but the process of creation is not always recognizable to the human mind. It is concealed in the mystery, expanding and drawing all that is created into the forms of creation itself. The essence of creativity is only one aspect of the divine soul! From the dust itself, there are infinite images and miracles that form from the surface alone. Every facet of the divine is a mystery in the process of development!

The power that makes a hero from a single sperm is the same power that opens the way for flight in a dream. Thoughts fly away and are overcome in the midst of the miracles of creation. We are being called into a dimensionless realm!

*Every moment, something new
is being created to develop our imagination!
Every moment, something is taken away
to leave room for new images to arrive!*

As the spirit develops into a physical being, the origin of the soul is forgotten, and man becomes exiled from his own deeper nature. Human beings either follow others who tell them what they should be doing, or they seem to have some direction of their own. Many heroes are created, and many idols are made for people to emulate and aspire to be just like them. Yet, following the path of someone else leads to a feeling of alienation inside the human heart and continues to deepen until one's own true path is discovered.

What causes man to lose touch with his own inner guidance? The answer seems to be different for each person, and it can be for any number of different reasons. The desire to have power, to be in control, or even to accumulate more possessions can all be major influences in the feeling of separation within the self. After experiencing the illusion of power, a feeling of arrogance develops, and it is easy to assume that one has made a success of life or that they understand what others do not.

**The fear of being judged by others develops doubt and can cause some people to go into seclusion, hiding away in a world of personal attachments. Rumi's image of us sitting in the bottom of the well congratulating ourselves, in the following poem, gives a humorous and yet sad image of clinging to a hiding place in the world, while holding on to illusions of safety.**

Love is what polishes the mirror of the heart to reflect the soul and motivates the lover to face the challenges of the obstacles to growth. Love constantly stimulates the heart to beat to keep the blood flowing, drawing each person in the direction of their unfolding and becoming.

*You are the essence of my existence.
Who am I? A mirror in your hand!
Whatever you do, I will do.
I am your irresistible reflection.*

When we cross the mythical river within us, we step into the flow and find our true self. We discover the spring of the spirit and remember who we really are. Rumi tells us to cross whatever mountain stands in our way and invites us to spread our wings in the freedom of the love that is already ours. Only love is the language that surpasses time and space and is understood and felt by everyone on a deeper level. It is in the freedom of love that we can discover an identity that is ours through grace.

# DİVAN OF SHAMS: POEM NO. 945

*The soul hears a call from within,
how long will you wander around?
Come back home.*

*You were born to live
at the height of intimacy.
Rise like the phoenix,
face our direction and soar.*

*You have been chained to shackles
made of water and mud.
Make an effort and break
the links, one by one by one.*

*Break free from this exile!
Come back home!
We are weary of this separation!
Make a move!*

*You are surrounded
with snippets and a ghostly mirage.
Your life is spinning
from many vain attempts.*

*Every cell in your body
is created to rise to challenges.
Your life is meant to confront
everything that holds you captive.*

*Wings of hope languish
from lack of use.
When wings dissipate and weaken,
life loses its value.*

*You are sitting at the bottom of the well,
not caring about salvation.*

Hey! Congratulations! Cheer yourself
in the dark abyss of a well gone dry!

Listen to the voice within calling to you,
Reach for eminence beyond your maturity!
You are not a child.
Don't cling to others to lead!

What is eminence of soul?
Is it not found in crossing the river in faith?
Hurry and cross over the chasm of doubt
into your promised home!

Why are you mincing water
in the grinder of passion?
When there is no substance,
you are only grinding arrogance.

God called the flora of the earth,
the Vanities of the World.*
Why rummage like animals in this flora
for what you cannot even digest?

Beware! The Wine has fermented!
Don't let it become sour!
Break the seal and prepare yourself
for a feast of sweetness!

Pay attention!
The Soul is here to reflect its own beauty.
Remove the tarnish of the flesh
and clear the mirror of your heart!

I am forbidden to reveal
the hidden mystery of life!
Reach deep within to discern
from the Source of all Life!

\* Passages from the Koran.

*Poem No. 945*

# SOUL OF THE SOUL

The soul is the power of existence, which lives within every body, yet the body itself is not capable of beholding it. The soul is eternal, divine, and limitless.

> Even though your body turns to dust,
> your soul goes to heaven.
> When the skin is torn apart,
> the essence does not die.
> Rumi's Masnavi

The soul is the expansive inner dimension of the body. It is the energy of divine intellect and consciousness that exists even without the body. Soul is the flow of life. It is the light that shines to make the image appear. It also guides the heart on the way to reach for union with the beloved.

**Even if the body becomes contaminated, the soul remains pure within the body.**

Soul is the mirror that reflects the divine beloved. Rumi describes it as half of a leaf from the rose garden of the beloved. The soul is the wholeness or fullness of Love.

> *What is soul?*
> *Half of a leaf*
> *from the rose garden of your grace.*
> *What is heart?*
> *A blossoming rose*
> *in the splendor of your presence.*

When the soul is permeated by grace, it is overpowered by love. Rumi calls it the soul of the Soul. It is total annihilation of the lover into the essence of love to the point that self is not apparent any more. The soul of the lover becomes concealed inside the soul of the beloved.

When the rose opens its veil to be caressed by the beloved, it is the energy breaking away to be in the flow of life and its expansion. The rose is not overwhelmed by its beautiful looks. It opens to continue expanding without any attachment. It becomes naked and vulnerable to surrender to the flow to experience something new as it does in the unfolding of spring.

When the energy of the soul of the Soul begins to expand, it reaches the soul of the lover who is longing to be touched. This is the touch that transforms. This is the touch that puts every flower in the garden in ecstasy, because they reach to be touched. The lover is touched from beyond the self. The soul of the lover is touched by its own essence or its own soul. It is a touch that makes one realize that life is to unfold in an unlimited garden that is sometimes like a burning fire, and other times, peaceful and calm. This is the nature of the flow of the soul into the soul of the Soul that becomes the guide for the lover.

> **Annihilation before physical death takes place when everything but the beloved dies in order to come back to life through the passage of love to live as the beloved.**
> Eyn al Ghozat

The energy of love moves in the direction of the essence of the beloved, which makes the lover feel safe in the embrace.

When the eyes and the heart are pure and filled with joy, the soul dissolves in the soul of the Soul. When that happens, the lover is not looking for heaven or the Garden of Eden any more. The soul of the Soul has increased the vision and the awareness of the heart. The lover is attracted and guided only toward the beloved.

> **The one who finds the way to the winehouse would be a fool to knock at any other door.**
> Hafiz

The constant flow in the direction of the beloved transforms the vision. The lover sees beauty in everything. The heavenly breath of the beloved offers energy to plants to grow and offers life to raise the dead. It removes the negative and the darkness from the face of the earth. The soul of the Soul is the guide to all who are lost and is the help to those who are impoverished and miserable.

The monarchs of the world become humble in the presence of the beloved. The life and the existence of the earth and the sky spring from the soul of the Soul. They are only a ring in the spiral that unfolds in the direction of the beloved.

> **The lover and the beloved**
> **live beyond time and space,**
> **for the universe is the ring on the door**
> **to the kingdom of the beloved.**
> Attar

To Rumi, the beloved is the master within all masters, the belief in all beliefs, the insight in every insight, the truth in every truth, the brightness in every light, and the soul inside every soul. The full meaning of the beloved is so much larger than any particular form it could take, for it encompasses the life and breadth of all form.

# DĪVĀN OF SHAMS: POEM NO. 1805

*Hidden like the soul,*
*you softly enter my soul.*
*You become my shimmering cypress,*
*the splendor of my life.*

*O soul of my soul!*
*Don't leave without me!*
*Don't move away from this lonesome body!*
*Don't withhold your radiance from my sight,*
*O glittering glory of my vision!*

*I will tear apart the seven skies!*
*I will cross the seven seas,*
*as your luring eyes gaze*
*into my bewildered spirit.*

*Ever since you entered my body,*
*doubt and belief are in my command.*
*Seeing you has become my faith;*
*your face is now my belief.*

*You have taken away my reason and my means.*
*You have stolen my appetite and my sleep.*
*Come back to your longing Jacob,*
*O my lost Joseph of Canaan!*

*Your grace permeated my soul!*
*I have become invisible to myself.*
*Your being is now*
*concealed inside my being!*

*O everlasting garden of my life,*
*the rose disrobes to be in your arms!*
*The jasmine is in ecstasy from your touch.*
*Every tree branch is pregnant with you!*

*One moment you set me on fire,
and the next I am calm among the roses.
You guide me gently into the light,
so my eyes would open to see!*

*You are the Soul before any other soul!
You are the Source before any other source!
You are the Beginning before all other beginnings!
You are the "I" before every other "I"*

*Since the dust is not my home,
I have no fear of turning to dust!
My limit is not this world,
for our union is beyond heaven!*

*All of my sighs and my cries
flow from the remembrance of your grace.
The scent of the king of my heart
bewilders me moment by moment!*

*My life, like a particle in the air,
has become separated from the light of your Sun!
O essence of earth, water, fire, and air,
how could I even exist without you?*

*O Salah Uddin,\* O king in my life,
you fill my needs; you grant my wishes!
You don't ask for my submission,
for you are higher than my possibilities!*

---

\*Salah Uddin Zarkub was a common and simple goldsmith, a dedicated supporter and patron of Rumi and one of his closest and most loyal friends and disciples. Salah Uddin's daughter was married to Rumi's eldest son. It is said that Rumi created this poem while mourning at Salah Uddin's death. Salah Uddin's selflessness in service was an expression of compassion that Rumi must have recognized as the depth of love of the soul that he praises in these verses.

Poem No. 1805

# Ultimate Reality

What Rumi calls the soul of the Soul is the true nature of reality. Some call it God; others call it the creator, the essence or the sustainer of the universe. Sufis call it *Hagh* or the ultimate reality. It is the substance of the whole existence. It is the very essence of the energy of life. It is the only reality, the purest light.

To the Sufis, the concept of *Hagh* means, God is everything, which is different from the idea of everything is God. This means whatever is visible to our eyes is insignificant, for it does not exist in the ultimate reality. It only seems real to us when seen from a relative perspective. Only God exists in reality, an inclusiveness that embraces us all.

> **Even though creation is different from the creator, in reality, the creator is the creation itself. Everything evolves from one reality. God is the only reality, and it is God who manifests in all realities.**
> 
> Ibn e Arabi

Rumi frequently uses the word *Hagh* to mean the creator and the originator of everything that is manifested in the universe. The celestial purity and the power of *Hagh* is reflected throughout the entire existence. We are the manifestation and reflection of that existence.

> *Since the light of the ultimate reality has no opposite,*
> *we are not able to see or detect it with our human eyes.*

Rumi considers it foolishness to give attention or to yield to anything but the ultimate reality. Surrendering to the divine power is the foundation for pride and honor. Ultimate reality has no limit and is without end. It is within the mystery that we reach for what is truly eternal.

> *Don't expect your life to have limitation.*
> *You are the quality of Hagh, which has no limit or end.*

*Hagh* in Rumi's poetry is union with the soul. It is the spring of life and the ocean of abundance. It is the power of all beings and the headspring or the source of purity. Hidden grace and divine justice are gifts of the ultimate reality. The whole universe is in need of *Hagh*, but *Hagh* is without need. Generosity and forgiveness flow from the ultimate reality as an expression of the divine nature.

Everything beautiful and joyful originates from the ultimate reality. Stunning flowers grow in a salt desert, dust becomes pregnant, treasures develop in the heart of the mountain, pearls are nurtured in the depth of the sea, and weariness and grief leave man's mind during sleep. The sun, the stars, and the moon revolve freely, while the mind of man is entangled with trickery and deceit, all through the power of *Hagh*.

Becoming intimate with *Hagh* is to reach beyond earthly influence and be free from all who claim to be agents or messengers of the ultimate reality.

> *When you become intimate with Hagh,*
> *you are already beyond saints.*
> *Remove the veil from*
> *the face of your veiled virtues.*

The following poem is placed as the first poem in the *Divan of Shams*. The identifying number of the poem has nothing to do with its context, and it is only based on the alphabetical order of the rhyming word in each line. It is quite interesting that the very first poem starts with Rumi's use of the word, *Hagh*. He consistently uses descriptions such as bounty of grace, presenter of hope, pulse of every heart, creator of every desire, and the sole giver of the soul throughout his verses.

The ultimate reality is the power that makes the heart to beat. It is the beloved who fills every thought, who creates every desire, and who satisfies every need! It invites one to surrender to joy beyond the rational influence of the self!

Rumi speaks of the deeper invitation that is always waiting for everyone to answer. It is to live, to take a chance, to risk it all, and to have faith and believe that it is true! Drop the burdens of constant thinking and continuously searching for approval. Live the incredible joy of every moment that *Hagh* has developed so graciously for us!

## DĪVĀN OF SHAMS: POEM NO. 1

*O sudden resurrection!*
*O countless blessings!*
*O blazing fire*
*in the jungle of thoughts!*

*Today, you arrive with laughter*
*to break open the jail.*
*You have arrived*
*as the bounty and grace*
*to all who long for you!*

*You are the proprietor of the sun.*
*You are the presenter of hope.*
*You are the cause and the effect.*
*You are the beginning and the end!*

*You give a pulse to every heart.*
*You adorn every thought.*
*You create every desire,*
*and you satisfy every need.*

*O giver of my soul!*
*You are the delight of every action and awareness;*
*all others are plans and pursuits.*
*One is the illness; the other is the cure.*

*We fall in the trap and become cynics.*
*We become hostile with the innocents.*
*Sometimes a carved idol makes us drunk,*
*other times, the taste of bread and butter.*

*Feel the thrill and forget about the cause.*
*See the sweetness,*
*and let go of reason.*
*Don't make such a fuss over your plight*
*for a loaf of bread and a morsel to chew!*

*You come up with hundreds of colorful gimmicks
to master the light
and command the darkness.
In the midst of the battle,
you conduct a marvelous act not seen before!*

*Rubbing the ear of the soul in secret,
dodging everyone with excuses,
shouting to God to liberate you,
I swear to God, they are all nonsense!*

*Be silent! I am in a big hurry
rushing to the festival.
Put down the paper! Break the pen!
The Winegiver is here!
Let's get drunk by drinking joy!*

# SPIRITUAL REDEEMERS

The word *Rend* in Farsi refers to a person who is unrestrained like a free thinker or a libertine. When used in mystical poetry, it is in reference to those who have eliminated every attachment to the physical world and have reached a level of supremacy in spiritual achievement. Rends are spiritual redeemers who are absorbed in *Hagh* or the ultimate reality and manifestation of Love. They have exceeded the limitations of rules and restrictions and have stepped beyond the man-made laws.

The messages that come through rends help to develop humanity. Their mission is to guide human beings to reach for the level that the original man, Adam, was created to reach before he became entangled in worldly matters.

**Rends are here to unite people and transform mankind into a nation of love and compassion. They show the way to live both a divine life and a creative life, which is the whole focus and intent of creation.**

Life is about connection, expansion, and about fusion. Yet, man uses his individual wisdom to draw on reason for discerning thoughts in order to experience comparison to make judgments. The logical mind usually wants to pull apart the web of life by focusing on the self. Rends are the selfless spiritual redeemers, whose mission is to bring the fullness to the web of life.

> Although I am a rend,
> I am not a thief, a bandit, or a robber.
> I am not a man of hypocrisy and pretense.
> I am free from honor and disgrace,
> free from good and evil.
> Since I do not appear like any of these,
> I behave like a rend.
>
> Attar

Rends are the great beings in our physical world who are directly connected with the spiritual realm. Their wisdom is guided by the divine intellect. Rends see life through its limitless dimension. They are the reflection of the divine command, delivering joy, freedom, and justice to earth.

Rends are not linked to anything that would separate people from one another, or that would divide humanity because of dissimilar belief systems. On the contrary, rends guide us to transform all our impurities so we would move toward unity.

Rends keep the development of the earth alive. They are the protectors of humanity, and because of that, they are deeply connected with our lives. Rends serve as the watchmen over the essence of existence.

*I am the drunken rend filled with love.*
*I am drowned in ecstasy in the circle of rends.*

Rends set aside their own thought and reasoning to invite the flow of the passage of divine intellect and divine wisdom to be expressed through them. They have given up focusing on their own life to exist in a timelessness of the mystery of the unknown.

Rends, unlike rulers, refuse to set themselves above anyone else. Early Persian kings and rulers such as Cyrus and Darius were considered rends who were directly connected with human life. They were not like ordinary kings ruling over their subjects. The king was an expression of life that flowed into the heart, the brain, and the wisdom of everyone.

Being a rend is not something one can choose to be. It develops through a concentrated journey of testing and discovery.

*When our faith becomes all love,*
*we enter into greatness.*
*When we come from that essence,*
*our physical being and everything else benefits from it.*
*We live in abundance.*

*From the center of that fullness,*
*Shams shines from Tabriz,*
*and our spirits are immersed into a sea of light.*
*We become pearls that fill the sea.*

Rends live as a part of the wholeness of existence! They are not involved with identity of details, the dates, or the facts of life. They are directly connected to the source of existence itself. Rumi himself was experiencing this existence through poetry, music, and whirling dances. Jesus experienced it through his discourses, teachings, healings, and the heightened ways it flowed through him during his time on earth. Light spreads naturally through each person, because its nature is to spread for everyone and everything.

**Truth exists in the manifestation of all who live by it. If the manifestation is isolated or set apart as the truth by itself, it immediately becomes separated from the Truth. The truth exists prior to the manifestation and is expressed through creation, for it is not relative to a particular view or belief.**

All creation is the expression of life coming through those who are open to creative flow. That is the freedom inherent in the divine command.

# DIVAN OF SHAMS: POEM NO. 2277

*There are a few rends on this side*
*sheltered in the heart.*
*Divine light illuminates the soul*
*as it beams through the ceiling of the heart.*

*Every rend shines like Venus among the stars.*
*Each particle radiates like a sun.*
*Our sun and the stars are bewildered*
*circling about them like atoms.*

*These redeemers, whose soul rests in the heavens,*
*have given their hearts*
*and yielded their reasoning.*
*They are rulers and monarchs*
*without banners or army.*

*You have exhausted many mounts,*
*circling the world.*
*Journey inside your soul*
*and discover the divine soul.*

*With such heavenly gifts*
*as grace and goodness,*
*behold the obedient ones*
*drowned in the command.*

*Their chests are pure as the mirror,*
*clear of all imperfections.*
*Their hearts are the center of the universe*
*embracing the throne of the King.*

*The abundance of sweetness and wine*
*and everything else in this world*
*flows in serenades and ecstatic songs*
*pouring from their lips.*

*If I could be free of reasoning,
as I was last night,
I would not be concerned with disturbance,
and I could continue
to express the rest in my selflessness.*

*But for now, I become silent,
for I am pawned for my ego,
until my heart is immersed again
in the ecstasy of love.*

*The sultan of sultans of the soul,
is Shams, the truth of Tabriz,
Every soul is a sea in him,
and every body blossoms
in longing for his love.*

# BREAKING THE LOCK

The human being has been formed as the noblest of all creation and the pinnacle of divine expression. Man is life expressed out of the most benevolent love that has ever existed. Yet, he is walking around in a stupor, unaware of who he is, how elegantly he has been made or how he is created to receive the gift of the fullness of life!

> **Man is the manifestation of the divine essence.**
> **Man is the summation of all divine attributes.**
> **Man is the ultimate worth of the entire existence.**
> **Man is the convincing proof of divine power.**
> Shah Nemat Allah Vali

Man's challenge is to reach into the depths of his soul to break the hold of the darkness within him. Should anyone choose not to surrender to the divine will, he would not benefit from the gift of this planet or from the gift of life itself.

**We are summoned as a community of created beings to rise into the fullness of all that we are and to help transform the earth into the paradise of unity it was intended to be.**

Rumi invites us to stand up and break apart all the worldly threats that have imprisoned us and are still destroying the divine existence we have been offered. He is inviting us to challenge all that cheapens, damages or belittles our inheritance of life. We need to proclaim and celebrate this exquisite garden of earth and to live as we were meant to live, which is living together in the oneness and fullness of love.

The poem in this chapter was delivered by Rumi, after he spent ten days in solitude to receive the hidden messages through his heart. This was followed by a lengthy period of rumination, according to the account of Aflaki, one of Rumi's principal hagiographers.

Hessam Uddin, a close disciple of Rumi and his number one devout follower, stated that one day his master, Rumi, came to his house and asked for a completely secluded and private room where he would have no disturbances. Hessam said that he prepared a room for him where the door and the windows were completely covered. He was then asked to bring as many sheets of quality paper as he could find in the market. Hessam brought him hundreds of sheets of the finest paper.

After the papers were delivered, Rumi asked Hessam to begin to write down what he said. He dictated both in Farsi and in Arabic, and Hessam wrote it down as he delivered it to him. After each page was completed, Rumi would ask Hessam to read it to him very deliberately in a loud, clear voice. At times, he would ask Hessam to read a certain passage again. After he would finish reading, the paper was to be set down in front of Rumi. This process went on almost continuously for a period of ten days.

After the ten days, Rumi asked Hessam to heat up the water for his bath. The bath at that time was made of baked clay in a way that one could stand up in it with water up to the level of their chest. The water in the tub was heated by wood or charcoal burning under the tub. To get inside the tub, there was an opening on the upper side just wide enough for a person to slide through it. Hessam said Rumi picked up all the written pages and stood by the fire and burned them page after page. As he would place them in the fire, flames would build up higher and higher, and Rumi would smile and repeatedly say that they came from a mysterious source, and they would return to that same source.

Hessam said that he tried to save a few of the pages, but the master noticed and told him no, that these messages were only for Rumi and that no one else was to learn about them. The revelation of mystery is not suitable for everyone. Listening to the words requires a certain soul that has been prepared for it.

Once the pages were completely burned, Rumi got into the bath with his clothes and his turban still on, and he stayed there for hours and hours through the night to purify his soul, his body, and all his attachments. Next morning, at dawn, he emerged with only his head out of the opening, and it was then he started to utter the words of the poem reflected in this chapter.

In the following poem, Rumi is representing and speaking for the human

*Breaking the Lock*

being. He is empowering all humans to claim the universe; to rise up and realize that we are very special beings in this world. We are all meant to come together to preserve all that is good around us and all that is good in each other. He is holding up the mirror for us to see the highest capabilities in ourselves, which he often describes and proclaims in so many of his verses. He calls us to divine action to break apart all that threatens the elegance of life!

Staying in the tub for a long period of time could have been for the purpose of purifying himself of whatever was left from his rigid beliefs. Even his clothing had to be purified. It may have been a way to experience a total cleansing. It would mean getting rid of all that is not helping in the path of living through the heart.

# DĪVAN OF SHAMS: POEM NO. 1375

I have returned in a new day of celebration
to break open the lock of the prison
and to demolish the claws and the teeth
of the wheel that is grinding the people.

I have returned to put out
the fiery flames of the seven stars
that devour the earthlings
and deflate the winds of arrogance.

I have flown here from the empire
of the boundless King as a falcon
to break apart the owl that preys
on the parrot of this ruined monastery.

I have made a vow from the beginning
to sacrifice my life for the King.
If I break my vow and my promise,
may the back of my soul be broken.

I am standing as a keen supporter
with the sword in my hand
to break the neck of all who rebel
against the Sultan's high command.

Don't be upset if you see
the garden of the rebellious is greener,
for I will always break their roots
in a mysterious way.

I will not break anything but oppression
and the cruelty of brutal tyrants.
If there is even one ounce of goodness,
I would be condemned if I break it.

*Wherever there is a ball,
the union with the striking club causes it to roll.
I will break the ball
that does not surrender to the blow.*

*I have remained at the royal feast,
for I have seen the kindness of the Sultan.
I have become a pebble on the royal path,
so I could break the leg of Satan.*

*From a pebble, I became a mine
when I surrendered to the King.
Don't try to weigh me, for I will
break apart and smash your scale.*

*Why would you allow a drunken
libertine like me in your home?
This means you are not aware
that I will break this as well as that.*

*If the guard stops me for being drunk,
I will throw the wine in his face.
If the gatekeeper grabs my arm
to keep me away, I will break his hand.*

*If the wheel does not revolve around my heart,
I will break its axle and its source.
If the universe becomes destructive,
I will break the turning of the revolving wheel.*

*You are the one who spread the table
and invited me as your special guest.
Why do you punish me if I break
a piece of bread at your feast?*

*Nay, Nay! My place is the head of the table!*
*I am your highly honored guest.*
*I am offering the special wine to others,*
*to help them break their shame.*

*O you, in the heart of the Soul*
*inspiring my poetry,*
*if I remain quiet and stay silent,*
*I am afraid I might break your command.*

*The wine that comes from*
*Shams of Tabriz moves me to ecstasy.*
*I become fearless and move with passion*
*to break the spine of the universe.*

# GIFT OF LOVE

Love and devotion are the two main elements that are the core of Sufi practices. Devotion is the stance of the heart in surrendering to God, or in the surrendering of the lover to the beloved. It is an opening in the heart to allow divine grace to flow through it.

> **How long will you continue knocking on an open door hoping that someone will open it?**
> Rabia

Devotion is the act of surrendering the ego and rational mind to the mysterious energy of love. It is to give the self completely to the beloved and to welcome whatever flows from that transformation. It is the dissolving of the lover into the beloved until nothing is left of the lover as a separate entity. Mystics guide us to surrender, knowing that we are sheltered within by a power far greater than our own ego and mind.

Mystics explore the path that leads to the beloved, and they reveal what is necessary to journey on that path until the purity of the inner nature is revealed.

> **Amazing! How could it be that the one whose heart has been pierced by love has the remainder of anything of the self to be bewildered? Love consumes everything of the lover. It numbs the senses, drives away the human intellect and astonishes every thought. What happens to bewilderment, and who is left to be bewildered?**
> Ibn e Arabi

Rumi refers to the gift of love as polishing the mirror of the heart so the tarnish of the ego-self is completely cleansed. When the lover has surrendered the ego-self, the mirror of the heart is polished to reflect only the beloved.

When the lover has completely lost the ego and the rational mind is broken down, the beloved appears and the madness of love takes over. At this point, the ego-self of the lover is annihilated, and the lover exists only for the beloved, but the beloved does not necessarily exist only for the lover. The beloved exists for all lovers. Yet, the lover accepts whatever the beloved desires without any expectations or personal demands.

The lover who is immersed in divine love, moves beyond the mundane life and becomes aware of the higher realities of divine consciousness. From then on, he carries the feeling of connectedness with anyone who attracts it. He can no longer express any feeling that might invalidate his love. Such character development would flow beyond the limitation of the self into an external manifestation and a new expression appears in his social relationships. The heart that is filled with divine love is filled with love for everything and everyone. The lover, who is dedicated to the divine beloved as the energy and the essence of the source of all life, will also be dedicated to other human beings.

The love and devotion of a Sufi is not based on any condition or limitation. A Sufi has no wish or demand other than longing to be one with the Beloved.

> The lover does not see this world,
> for the lover is bewildered in a different world.
> No one understands the lover's language,
> for the lover speaks with a different tongue.
> No one understands that tongue, yet
> everyone has a deeper connection with it.
>
> Attar

Rumi often chooses to speak of *Hagh*, the ultimate reality, in terms of love as both the beloved and the lover. Love refers to the mysterious essence, while the lover and beloved refer to the creation and creator or the human and divine. In wholeness there is only one reality, which is love, and it manifests as both the lover and the beloved.

> *Love and the lover are one, my dear.*
> *Do not even imagine that they are two halves.*

This concept of love as one reality is the heart of mysticism and the soul and center of life. Rumi's love is a transcending state of the lover or the one who is the seeker of the divine beloved. The *Divan of Shams* is the devoted expression of love to the manifesting beloved, using Shams of Tabriz as a symbol of the ultimate reality or *Hagh*.

> *Love builds the mirror of the heart,*
> *and devotion builds the temple of the soul.*

True lovers transform the self and are defiant against pretense, hypocrisy, and conceit. They do not promote their ego-self. Rumi clears the mirror and calls the beloved into the temple through love and through his sacred songs and dance. The beloved opens the arms of love and wraps the lover in a warm embrace drawing his whole being close to his heart. It is as if the beloved is answering the longing and has come to share the treasure of love with the lover through the beauty of divine intimacy.

The following poem expresses the deeper reason why love appears to us as a gift that inspires and invites us to enhance our own lives, as well as to be willing to share it with others. Love finds its way into our hearts and minds and souls, and it pushes and forces all that is not love out of our inner world.

Love comes to hold us in those welcoming arms to spread our joy; draws us close and watches over us to celebrate the wonder of living in this world! Love goes before us, walks beside us, follows after us and moves beneath to hold us up. It is also above us, and beyond us guiding and preparing the way. Love like this is everyone's deepest longing, even when unknown and unspoken.

The gift of Love is the greatest gift to the world. It is meant for every heart to receive it but not to project it on an icon. The gift of Love is not to invest all hopes in some particular person that can never sustain or hold those deeper longings for someone else.

# DIVAN OF SHAMS: POEM NO. 322

*I have come to take you by the ear
and pull you into myself.
I have come to steal your heart and mind
and to place you in my soul.*

*O blossoming tree!
I have come as a fine spring
to hold you in my arms
and softly spread your joy.*

*I have come to offer you
splendor in this place,
to lift you above heaven,
like the songs of lovers.*

*I have come, because you stole
a kiss from a carved idol.
Give it back with grace,
or I will take you away!*

*What is the rose? You are the rose!
You are the divine message!
If no one can recognize it,
I know, because I am you!*

*You are my soul; you are the flow in my soul!
You grant me wholeness!
Expand and reveal your brilliance,
so I can place you in my heart!*

*You are my prey; you are my catch,
even if you have leaped out of my snare!
Come back into the snare.
If you don't, I will lead you in.*

*The lion says,*
*you are a wondrous deer; be gone!*
*Why do you run in my wake so swiftly?*
*Don't you know, I will tear you to pieces!*

*Accept the wound and move forward,*
*for you are the valiant shield.*
*Yield only to my bowstring,*
*so I can bend you to my bow.*

*There are thousands of stages*
*from the limits of dust to man.*
*I have taken you from place to place;*
*I will not leave you along the way!*

*Say nothing! Don't let your blood boil!*
*Don't raise the lid of the pot!*
*Simmer with joy and be patient*
*until I have developed you.*

*You are born of a lion,*
*hidden within a deer.*
*I will take away your cover*
*and transform you at once.*

*You are my ball*
*running at the command of my bat.*
*Even though I make you run,*
*I always follow behind you.*

# SILENCE OF LOVE

God is the name given to the infinite and eternal energy that is always creating and is beyond boundaries, time, place, words and beyond all comprehension. While God is not known through the mind, we discover a deep well and a fountain of love inside our hearts through which God may be experienced in a divine touch igniting us with love.

**Silence is the ultimate presence of God to all that is created as well as all that has not yet been created.**

We keep a vigil of love in reverent silence in response to the overwhelming gift of love that has offered us life. Unable to hold it inside, we break out in praise and celebration of the beauty of that love.

Rumi embodied the expression of love in a way that elevated earth to heaven. He became part of the great mystery and the union that awakens the heart from a deep sleep to reveal the infinite truth of who we are.

*In the beginning was the Word, and the Word was with God, and the Word was God* is a powerful metaphor alluding to the great silence rather than spoken words. In the beginning, there was no one to speak. It was a process unfolding in silence or a divine decree that manifested in a creative result. This is an indication that the divine power, or the power of creativity, is a profound intention arising from silence. Mystics consider this process the manifestation of love.

**The Infinite is expressed through Silence.**

The greatest of human achievements have not evolved from the words expressed by a person manifesting greatness, but from the depth of the silence of pure intention.

The essence of love and creativity exists in silence and not in the words that are derived from the rational mind. Every word evolves from silence, every sound proceeds from silence, and everything that is created has originated from silence.

Words can sometimes dissipate power rather than strengthen it. In many cases, the loss of power is the result of talking about the intention before it has manifested.

> **There are two kinds of speech and two kinds of silence.**
> **Speech is either true or false;**
> **silence is the result of achieving a goal or neglecting it.**
> **When truth is spoken, words are better than silence,**
> **but when words are fabricated or untrue, silence is better than speech.**
> Al Hajwiri

Life is illuminated when the lips are closed and the heart expresses itself. Silence enhances power. It is the pride of the humble and the humility of the proud. It is the zenith of merit for the brave and the haven of security for the coward. Silence is the wisdom of fools and the discretion of the wise.

Silence is the basis for the development of character. It is the mystery and the voice within the heart that leads to reverence, patience, self-control, endurance, and courage.

> **Two actions are identified with foolishness:**
> **Silence when it is time to speak;**
> **speak when it is time to be silent.**
> Saadi

Rumi has given more value to silence for those on the path of enlightenment than other mystics. Many of the poems in the *Divan of Shams* end with the phrase, be silent, or some other descriptive phrase about being silent. His most mystical poems and those with deeper meanings often reflect the importance of silence. Perhaps some of the best expression in his poetry is when he tells himself to be silent. He does this when he feels the emergence of the rational mind interfering with his ecstatic state. He usually stops the poetry and goes into silence when that happens.

**Poetry for Rumi is the prelude to silence.**

To Rumi nothing is worth saying if what is said is not spoken out of love that flows freely through the heart to guide what is being said. In fact, poetry to him is conversation with love. It is in silence that love most easily finds the way to the heart. It is in silence that love is given the freest passage. When that happens, the expression of the message has the perfect clarity of truth. If we open our mouths to speak, and our words do not come from love, then we should say nothing.

Silence is pure essence, while talking is like a cover surrounding the essence. The deep ecstasy of the spiritual journey harbors the beauty that is hidden inside. Silence has many concealed advantages. The simplest one relieves apprehension and doubt and frees a person to embrace an inner peace.

> *I am a mirror! I am a mirror!*
> *I am not a person of words.*
> *I am revealed when*
> *your eyes become listening ears.*

There is a sacred silence inside everyone where a divine conversation can be heard. Be silent and listen to the whispers of love within the heart that long to be expressed and feel the tranquility and freedom love can bring.

> **Mystics who have received the divine wine**
> **have learned many secrets and kept silent.**
> **All who are truly aware of the mystery**
> **have closed and sealed their lips.**
> Rumi's Masnavi

Careless thoughts can take the form of words that pour out of the mouth every day. Thought has an energy that is carried with words. If the thought is negative, it goes out like an arrow and finds its mark in whoever might be in its path. Words can find soft vulnerable flesh and sting and cause pain, leaving wounds that can harm and steal the joy from the life of others.

Man has the creative power to send out thoughts that inspire and heal and warm the heart. Love is the cure for those wounds. Love has the healing power to help anyone forgive cruelty, to heal the inner wounds, and to find a way to transform the negative hurt that is carried inside.

*Silence of Love*

*A deep silence overcomes me,*
*and I wonder why I ever thought*
*to utter words.*

An important reason for silence is to conceal the mystery. Revealing the secrets to those who don't have the capacity to receive and understand often leads to adversity and conflict. Rumi's idea is to be so careful that we even hide the secrets from the walls and doors. The mystery is to be revealed only to those who are capable of holding the deeper truths silently within their hearts.

What matters in life is what is true and moments that are real. When love is felt and experienced, a connection is made whether it is with another person or when feeling the presence of divine love. Pure love is everything, and it flows from a deep and sacred silence that protects and guards the mystery.

Silence is the dwelling place of creation. It holds the mystery and surprise of all that is created. What is underneath the phrase *to say nothing or to be silent* is the longing for love.

# DĪVĀN OF SHAMS: POEM NO. 2219

*I am devoted to love.*
*Speak to me of nothing but love.*
*Only talk of sweetness and light,*
*or say nothing.*

*Don't talk about scarcity and pain.*
*Speak only of abundance.*
*If you have no awareness of it,*
*don't bother, say nothing.*

*A beautiful madness took over me last night.*
*Love whispered, I'm here.*
*Don't cry; don't tear up your robe.*
*Say nothing.*

*O Love, I said,*
*I am worried about other things!*
*There are no other things*
*beyond love, say nothing.*

*I will reveal to you the secrets!*
*Nod your head that you hear me.*
*Except for that,*
*say nothing.*

*Love, like life, flows*
*through the heart.*
*Feel the thrill of the flow*
*and say nothing.*

*O heart! I asked,*
*What is this enchanting flow?*
*This is beyond what you can grasp!*
*Give it up; say nothing.*

*Is this mysterious attraction an angel
or a human being?
This is beyond the angels
and all beings, say nothing.*

*Tell me what it is?
I am losing my mind.
Lose your mind.
Lose your control; say nothing.*

*You are sitting in this house
filled with phantoms and images.
Move out! Let go of your
obsessions and say nothing.*

*O heart! Be like a gentle father.
Isn't this the description of God?
Yes, it is true, but promise me
to say nothing.*

# QUOTED MYSTICS AND SUFI MASTERS

**Abu Saeed Abolkheir**     128, 144
Abu Saeed was a Sufi mystic who lived about two hundred years prior to Rumi (967 - 1049). He was a well-respected spiritual leader and a major figure in the development of Persian Sufi poetry. His fame was widely spread throughout the Islamic world as far as Spain during his lifetime. Abu Saeed, however, referred to himself as "nobody, son of nobody" expressing that his life had disappeared in the heart of God.

**Aflaki, Shams Uddin Ahmad**     19, 111, 156, 232
Little is known about Aflaki's life except that he was a Sufi historian who lived during the fourteenth century. He was a disciple of Chelebī Emīr 'Ārif, a grandson of Rumi, who commissioned him to write a collection of anecdotes related to Rumi's life known as *Manaʾqib al Arfin*. Aflaki died in 1360.

**Al Hajwiri, Ali ben Osman**     244
Also known as Sheikh Ali al-Hajwiri, he was a Sufi sage, a writer and a scholar of Islamic doctrine. He lived almost a century before Rumi and was a major contributor in spreading the Islamic beliefs in Southern Asia. Al Hajwiri was born in Ghazna and died in Lahore in 1077. His most famous work is *Kashf al Mahjub* (Unveiling of the Veiled), which was the first Farsi treatise on Sufism. His main idea was that true understanding of God is a silent one.

**Al Jili, Abdul Karim**     38
A descendent of the great saint and founder of the Qadiri dervish order, 'Abdul Qadir al Jilani. Al Jili was born in Baghdad in 1306. The only information about his life is found through his own writings of more than twenty books. His most outstanding work is *Al Insan al Kamel*, the Universal Man. It is a description of the appearances of an absolute being as the divine essence and developing contemplative states in the path of divine Union. Al Jili died in 1403.

**Al Jurjani, Ali ibn Muhammad**     182
Al Jurjani or Gorgani (1340 – 1413) was a theologian who wrote numerous books on Islam, which all but thirty of them have been destroyed. The most

valuable among his remaining books is the Dictionary of Islamic terms, which includes simple definitions and many Sufi references. A copy of his *Kitab al-ta'rifat*, commentary in manuscript, has also survived and is available in the University of the Punjab Library, Lahore, Pakistan.

**Ansari, Khajeh Abdollah**     69, 118, 177, 187
Ansari (1006 – 1088) was a celebrated Persian Sufi and a distinguished literate man who wrote several books about mysticism, philosophy, and Islam in Farsi and Arabic. He was born in Herat, which is why he is known as the "Pious of Herat". Ansari was the originator of a literary style called *Mona'jat*, Litanies, a form of rhythmic prose that is intimate invocation addressed to God. Ansari's famous work is *Manazil as-Sairin*, A Guide to Spiritual Stations of the Sufi path, which became fundamental work for the development of Sufi doctrine.

**Attar, Farid Uddin**     19, 20, 21, 33, 45, 70, 83, 85, 98, 106, 124, 135, 139, 151, 162, 188, 208, 220, 227, 239
Attar (1142 – 1220) is one of the most well-known Sufi mystic poets of Persia who was murdered by the Mongols. His great work, *Mantiq ut-Tair*, the Conference of the Birds, is a long allegory of the soul's search for divine truth. Among his many other books *Tadkhirat al-Awliya*, Biographies of the Saints, is another major work in Sufi literature. Rumi met Attar as a child, and this great mystic's works were a source of inspiration to him throughout his life. Rumi has referred to Attar and Sana'i several times in his poetry, for he held them both in high esteem. Perhaps the best introduction to Attar is by Rumi, who says:

> *Attar roamed the seven cities of love.*
> *I'm still in the bend of an alley.*

**Bastami, Bayazid**     25, 29, 67, 202
Also known as Bayazid e Bastami (804 - 874), was a Persian Sufi who had a great influence on Sufi mysticism and was one of its most important early teachers. He was the first mystic to emphasize the importance of ecstasy, or what he called drunkenness as a means of union with God. He was the first mystic to discuss *fana fi Allah*, Annihilation of the Self in God. Bastami's discourses about the unity of being and the concept of divine love eventually formed the core of Sufi doctrine. Prior to his death, someone asked him his age. He replied, I am four years old. I was veiled for seventy years. I became

unveiled only four years ago.

**Eyn al Ghozat**   40, 46, 172, 219
Eyn al Ghozat was born in the western Persian town of Hamadan in 1098. He was a well-known scientist and a judge who turned to writing mystical concepts. Among his writings, *Zubdat al-Haqhighat*, Essence of Truth, the *Maktubat*, Epistles, and *Tamhidat*, Essays, are the most eminently known. He was a fearless mystic who was finally executed and burned for the charge and crime of blasphemy. He was thirty-three years old when he was killed in 1131.

**Ezz Uddin Kashani**   193
Kashani was an author and Sufi of the latter part of the thirteenth and early fourteenth century, who died in 1334. Very little is known about Kashani's life. His most well-known work is *Estelahat al Sufieh*, a valuable manual of mystic ideas, which contains useful information about the expressions and idioms of the Sufis. This book is a valuable text for the scholars of Sufi studies.

**Gheisari, Ibn Davoud**   98
There is very little information about Gheisari, except that he was a student of the Sufi master Molla Abdul Razagh and that he died in 1349. His best known work is *Sharh e Fusus*, Analysis of the Seals, a fifteen-volume interpretation of Ibn e Arabi's *Fusus al-Hikam*, which is considered by many as the most important classical text of Islamic mysticism.

**Hafiz**   11, 19, 34, 44, 45, 84, 107, 119, 124, 171, 178, 182, 183, 219
Also spelled in English as Hafez, is the most celebrated lyric poets of Persia. Hafiz was born in Shiraz around 1320 and died there in 1389. His real name was Shams Uddin Mohammad, but he took Hafiz as his literary name. As it is with most other mystics, not much is known about his life except that he served as a court poet to several rulers of Shiraz. His poems are notable for their unaffected metaphors, rhythmic flow, and his use of the most delicate poetic images and profound expressions. His famous work is his *Divan*, a collection of nearly five hundred ghazals that combines exalted spirituality with vivid sensuality. Hafiz was not only a poet, but also a great Sufi mystic and a scholar of the religious sciences, literature, and philosophy. His poetry is focused on what he calls, ghazals worthy of the Beloved.

**Ibn e Arabi**     58, 223, 238

A celebrated Sufi mystic and philosopher, who was born in 1165 in Murcia, Spain and traveled extensively in the Islamic world in search of the Sufi path. He was a prolific writer and poet who claimed the way to God is through creative imagination and by reaching under the surface to the sacred presence that is hidden everywhere and in everything. Ibn e Arabi believed all faiths are equally valid to the mystic. He used to quote this verse from the Koran: *Wherever you turn, there is the face of God*. Ibn e Arabi was a highly influential writer who taught a unified and pluralistic spiritual vision. His best known works are *Fusus al Hikam*, the Seals of Wisdom, and *Al Futuhat al Makiyah*, the Secrets of Fasting. Ibn e Arabi died in 1240.

**Iraghi, Fakhr Uddin**     52, 119, 125, 134

Iraghi, whose name is also spelled Araqi, was a contemporary of Rumi and Ibn e Arabi. He was one of the paramount figures of the Eastern School, enriched by Hinduism and Buddhism, known for its musical and poetic expressions. Iraqhi developed an outstanding bridge between the metaphysics of Ibn e Arabi's Arabic and Rumi's Persian school of Sufism. The combination of the two appears in his *Lama'at*, Divine Flashes, rendered in the most exquisite poetry in Farsi, written in the language of love. Iraghi died in 1289.

**Lahiji, Shams Uddin Mohammad**     108, 167

Not much information is available on Lahiji, including the year of his birth. Apparently, he was a well-respected Sufi master and an outstanding philosopher of his times who lived in Shiraz. His fame rests largely on his commentary on the *Gulshan-e Raz* of Shabestari, a commentary that itself is one of the most illustrious texts among the works of mystics. According to what Lahiji writes in the introduction to his commentary, he began his writings in the year, 1472. The year of his death is not known precisely. It seems to have been sometime around 1494.

**Mansur al-Hallaj**     79, 146, 147

Mansur, also known as Hallaj (858 – 913), is one of the most controversial of the Persian mystics and one of the earliest Sufi masters who led his life as a wandering dervish. Mansur would often go into a trance, and during that state, he felt one with all creation as a whole and with God. During these courses, he uttered what is known as *shathiyyat*, the divine secrets, which were not to be revealed. He was finally accused of apostasy for claiming divinity for himself. He was pronounced as an apostate and was flogged, publicly mutilated, hung on the gallows, beheaded, and then his body was burnt. Hallaj was an inspiration to many subsequent Sufi mystics, including Rumi and Hafiz, for his courage and profound insight.

**Razi, Najm Uddin**     153, 213

Sheikh Abdollah ibn Muhammad Najm Uddin Razi was a famous thirteenth century Persian Sufi from Khwarezmia. He was one of the students of the great Sufi mystic, Najm Uddin Kubra, who was also the teacher of Rumi's father. When his master was murdered, he fled to Hamadan, then to Ardabil, and finally to Konya, where he settled with his contemporary fellow master, Rumi. There, he put the teachings of Najm Uddin Kubra into a book in Farsi called *Mersad ol Ebad*, the Path of God's Bondsmen. Razi died in 1247.

**Nasafi, Aziz -i**     88, 113, 171

Azīz ibn Mohammad al-Nasafī (known as Aziz-i Nasafi) was a Sufi mystic who flourished in Central Asia during the thirteenth century. Little is known about his personal life including the year of his birth or his death. His numerous writings in Farsi are in easy and didactic style, addressed to unknown dervish groups. Nasafi was a relatively prolific writer, and while his messages are not so original, they incorporate all the major elements of Sufi belief available during his era. Nasafi's major work, *Maqsad i aqsā*, the Most Sublime Goal, was one of the first Sufi works translated into Latin as well as English.

**Rabia al Adawiyyah**     238

Also known as Rabia, was a female mystic and one of the wonders of her time. Rabia was born in 717 and died in 801. She is the most important of the early Sufi poets who set forth the doctrine of mystical love. Rabia is noted for having gone into amazing spiritual trance state, uttering lofty sayings and elevating mystical verses. When she was asked by a Sufi master how she discovered the divine secrets, she responded, you know about how, and I know about how-less. Rabia was the first in a long line of female Sufi mystics.

**Ruzbehan Bagli Shirazi**     52, 194, 208
Ruzbehan (1128 – 1209) is known as *Shaykh-e Shattah*, Shouting Sheikh, because of his prolific religious affection and worship shouts. He was a poet, a mystic, and a Sufi master from Shiraz. He studied in his hometown and remained there throughout his life. Ruzbehan's best known book is *Abhar al Aasheqin*, Jasmine for Lovers, which is a guide for the seekers of human or divine love.

**Saadi**     19, 166, 244
Muslih Uddin Saadi, also spelled Sa'di, is one of the foremost poets of ghazals, the rhythmic poetry. He was born in 1213 in Shiraz and studied in Baghdad with Sohrevardi, a major Persian mystic. After his studies, Saadi traveled extensively before returning to Shiraz to settle in 1256. Saadi's two well-known books include *Gulistan*, The Rose Garden, a collection of mystical poems and *Bustan*, The Fruit Garden, an ethical dialectic text composed in the style of *Masnavi*. Saadi has also written many *ghasideh*, anecdotes, and mystical ghazals in Farsi and Arabic. He died in Shiraz and was buried there in 1293.

**Sana'i**     19, 73
Hakim Sana'i Ghaznavi is one of the earlier Sufi poets of verses filled with insightful emotion and profound mystical depth. He was born in the middle of the eleventh century and died in 1131. Sana'i is known as the first writer to introduce mysticism in Persian poetry. He was originally a court poet, who later turned to a mystic poet. Rumi claimed that Attar was his soul, and Sana'i was his eyes, and he developed his poetry after them. Sana'i presented mysticism as a philosophy of life. His Divan, a collection of poetry, was a popular text to study in the Sufi centers of the east. Sana'i wrote his most famous *Masnavi*, *Hadiqat-al-Haqiqa*, The Garden of Truth, at a very old age and died soon after its completion.

**Shabestari, Shaykh Mahmood**     105
Shabestari is considered one of the greatest mystics of the Sufi world. He was a renowned follower of Ibn e Arabi. He created poetry that was educational as well as mystical. He was born in 1250 in Shabestar, not too far from Tabriz, the birth place of Shams of Tabriz. Shabestari is the creator of the sublime book of poetry called *Gulshan e raz*, The Secret Garden, which has immortalized his name, and has had major influence on many Sufi poets.

Shabestari died in the year, 1320.

**Shah Nemat Ullah Vali    58**
A contemporary of Hafiz, Shah Nemat Ullah is a highly respected Sufi master, who started what is currently known as the *Nemat Ullahi* order, the most popular Sufi order throughout the world. Shah Nemat Ullah was born in Shiraz in 1350 and studied Sufi concepts and poetry in depth. It is written that he had memorized Ibn e Arabi's, *Fusus al Hikam*, the Seals of Wisdom, and knew various interpretations and commentary written about it. Aside from his Sufi teachings and poetry, Shah Vali developed a large center in Kerman where Sufis from all around were coming there for education and training. He died in 1430 and was buried near the city of Kerman where a Sufi shrine is built over his tomb.

**Sohrevardi, Shahab Uddin    202**
Sohrevardi was an influential Sufi philosopher who founded the School of Illumination, one of the most important doctrines in mystical concepts. He was born in 1155 in northwestern Persia. Although he lived a short life, Sohrevardi wrote numbers of books in Farsi and Arabic dealing with the subject of illumination. His major work, *Hekmat al Eshragh*, is a treatise on Oriental Philosophy, which is centered on the phenomenon of orient, or sunrise as the essential epiphany of being. Sohrevardi did not accept the view of religion as a law to be lived by without orientation toward the hidden Truth. This view caused his execution in 1191 on the charge of cultivating an inner esoteric level of meaning in the Koran.

# ABOUT THE AUTHOR

**Rassouli** is an artist, an author, and one of those beings, who Rumi describes in his verses as "a friend of the heart." The artistic being, who others call Rassouli, is like the play of the light on earth, for he is wildly and wonderfully creative, and he has mastered his medium to free him to be as creatively expressive as possible. He has a deep regard for the psyche and its mysteries, for the secrets of the subconscious and the unconscious, for the crowning capability of humanity. He surrenders to the process of spontaneous revelation in order to create.

He guides others to open their hearts and discover the secrets there, and he encourages the creative path that allows them to discover the way given to them to best be able to express their uniqueness.

Rassouli is an artist flowing in the living stream and energy of the creative wonder of a true mystic. He lives spontaneously through the experience of actively manifesting stunning, surprising, and sensuous artistic visions that exalt humanity and its potential! He paints and writes and speaks and shares his visions generously with others. He has written books on creativity, collaborated with other authors and artists to share his artworks, all of which are listed on many sites dedicated to him on the internet. There are countless articles in art magazines, newspapers, and recorded interviews on radio and television.

To try and capture the range of Rassouli's ever changing journey would be to describe it one day and have it out of date the next. He is an artist of light and the flickering shadows of passion and attraction streaming toward the brilliance of love pouring from the heart like vintage wine. Mystics cannot be contained, and if anyone tries, they will break through the bonds of whatever gets in the way of the energy attracting them to create!

Rassouli was raised in the continuing inspiration of the mystics since he was born. Rumi and Hafiz have been very dear to his heart throughout his life. Sharing the true genius of Rumi is a work of love, and Rassouli is totally dedicated to opening the scope of this brilliant man's contribution to the world in as many ways as possible, for it is only beginning to truly be revealed.

Websites:
www.Rassouli.com
www.AvatarFineArts.com
www.NewDawnCollections.com
www.FusionartInternational.com

ALSO AVAILABLE FROM BLUE ANGEL PUBLISHING

## Journey of Love Oracle Cards

**Guidebook by Alana Fairchild**
**Artwork by Rassouli**
**Poems by Richard Cohn**

Featuring 70 illuminating paintings by visionary artist Rassouli, the cards in *Journey of Love* are bursting with vibrant hues and stunning mystical depictions of feminine and natural beauty that help you connect deeply with the love that is at the very heart of everything in existence.

Accompanied by exquisite poetic verses by Richard Cohn and profound messages of guidance by Alana Fairchild, these cards are designed to assist you to find your authentic path through the opportunities for growth presented to you in all aspects of life, especially in your relationships, not only with others, but in your sacred relationship with yourself. Ask the oracle whatever it is you yearn to know, then be carried on a journey through the mists of time, where your answers await…

**Foreword by Jean Houston**

*ISBN: 978-1-922161-15-4*
*70 cards and 164-page guidebook, packaged in a hard-cover box.*

For more information
on this or any
Blue Angel Publishing® release,
please visit our website at:

www.blueangelonline.com